SHATTERED
SHEPHERDS

FINDING
HOPE IN THE MIDST OF
MINISTRY
DISASTER

STEVE SWARTZ

KRESS
BIBLICAL
RESOURCES

Kress Biblical Resources
www.kressbiblical.com

Shattered Shepherds: Finding Hope in the Midst of Ministry Disaster

ISBN 978-1-934952-22-1

Cover design by Kirk DouPonce, DogearredDesign.com
Interior design and typeset by Katherine Lloyd, theDESKonline.com

Dedication

To my faithful wife, Sylvia.

Never did a woman stand by her husband as you have by me. Thanks for your faith in the Lord and your faith in me. You have wept with him who weeps and rejoiced with him who rejoices. You have redefined the words "perseverance" and "determination." Thanks for your love for me, for our children, and for Christ's Church.

"Frustration, disappointment, and heartache are inevitable in pastoral ministry. Sheep are not always docile and cooperative, and there are plenty of wolves to contend with as well. Every church has people who seem to think criticism is a spiritual gift, and the pastor naturally gets the brunt of their complaints. Young men frequently leave the ministry in discouragement, and burnout is common among experienced pastors. Steve Swartz has experienced—and survived—church problems that would demoralize any pastor. He has written a compact but potent book that offers a wealth of straightforward biblical help and encouragement for fellow pastors struggling to get past ministry setbacks. This is a much-needed resource, and I'm glad to be able to recommend it."

—DR. JOHN MACARTHUR
President of The Master's Seminary and
Pastor of Grace Community Church in Sun Valley, California

"*Shattered Shepherds* aptly addresses the care of pastors and church leaders who have been badly hurt in the course of ministry. But rather than characterizing them just as victims, Steve lovingly encourages personal reflection and growth even while giving much-needed comfort to these wounded warriors. Steve's goal is to get these men back into the pulpit with renewed strength and soft hearts for God's people. Thoroughly biblical and immediately practical, this book will shepherd men and their wives back to the church of Jesus Christ."

—ALEXANDER STRAUCH, author of *Biblical Eldership*, international conference speaker, elder for over 40 years at Littleton Bible Chapel near Denver, Colorado.

"Many books instruct pastors in avoiding ministry problems; few deal with the aftermath of church disaster. Steve has touched this tender area of need for the church with *Shattered Shepherds*. Men of God who are nursing ministry-inflicted injury will find direction and hope to not only tend to bruises given by others but also honestly evaluate their own part in the disaster. In small easily-digested pieces, Steve feeds hope and honest shepherding to those decimated by ministry tragedy. Men who are still in the middle of a painful ministry will greatly benefit as well from the practical strategies for navigating those difficult waters. Most importantly, *Shattered Shepherds* is a call to godliness and holiness in the midst of ministry pain. Based in the solid rock of sound theology, men will be refreshed and bolstered so that they might serve Christ more humbly and more effectively."

—DR. GREGORY HARRIS, Professor of Bible Exposition at The Master's Seminary and Pastor of Lake Hills Community Church in Castaic, California

CONTENTS

IT'S TIME TO RUN AGAIN

I know you. You are the man who hears the classic sermon illustration often given jokingly to a chuckling congregation: "The church is made up of sheep, and sometimes sheep bite." And when you hear this, you think, "Sheep not only bite, but they kick, gossip, harm, send vicious letters, call secret meetings I didn't know about, plot evil, treat my family like outcasts, pay less than minimum wage, complain about everything, treat the church like it belongs to them, stand in the way of every good idea, and grow in bitterness against their leadership until I get humiliated and devastated in ways no one could really understand." I know you because I have stood in your shoes.

This book is for the pastor, elder, deacon, or other leader in the church who has invested his life and passion into his love for Christ's church—and been shot up for doing so by the very ones he serves. You have experienced the colorful gamut of emotions from crushing grief to teeth-grinding indignation. You've had 1,001 imaginary "I should have said" conversations with yourself, replaying painful interactions with others but with a happier, more victorious ending in which you overcome your opponent with unstoppable biblical logic. You have wept in the arms of your wife and had to put on a brave face for your children. You have had even the foundations of your understanding of the sovereignty of God shaken hard.

This book is not primarily for the one in the midst of a trial that is still on-going, although he may find this useful as a lesson in what to avoid. It is for the one who is sitting on the ash heap with Job, the devastation already complete, the loss total, and the possibility of recovery zero. It is for you who have asked questions like, "Why me?" "Why now?" "What has my ministry really accomplished?" "Am I done in ministry?" "Can I do this again?" "Can my family do this again?" "Can I love a congregation again?" "Can I trust church leaders again?"

I am taking a simple approach in this book: I'm going to tell you what to *stop* doing and what to *start* doing. Some of these are things you may not *feel* like stopping or starting, but you must. There are two ways to read this book. Like getting into cold water, you can ease your way in by skipping ahead and reading the "What You Must Start Doing" section first. Or you can just jump off the high dive and start right at the beginning with "What You Must Stop Doing." The choice is yours, but both must be done eventually.

I have written this book for two reasons. First, it is my hope that you gain traction on your road to feeling like a normal human being again. I know the bone-jarring impact that ministry disaster can have on every single aspect of your life, from your marriage to your blood pressure. Everything is touched.

The faster you get your bearings once again, the better off you and your family will be.

But I have a second reason, a more eternal reason. You are a minister of the gospel of Christ, with experience and training. The Church of Jesus Christ is crying out all over the world for faithful men who will lead the charge for sound doctrine, biblical preaching, and bold evangelism. The church desperately needs men to train other men (2 Tim 2:2). The enemy is prowling around devouring weak churches and weak believers, promulgating false doctrine, a seeker-sensitive cotton candy gospel, and mystical practices pawned off as legitimate worship. We are in a war and the Church cannot afford to have her most experienced officers sitting back behind the battle while the foot soldiers are getting clobbered. We need leaders, and we need them now. Sometimes in a war, even the wounded have to get up to fight.

In his classic declaration of victory, the Apostle Paul proclaimed, "I have fought the good fight, I have finished the race, I have kept the faith" (2 Tim 4:7). Paul often used the metaphor of the athlete as a picture of the Christian life. He uses this metaphor specifically of the gospel ministry, however, in 2 Timothy 2:5. If you think you cannot bear any more pain or heartache, consider Paul who asserted, "I endure everything for the sake of the elect, that they also may obtain the salvation that is in Christ Jesus with eternal glory" (2 Tim 2:10). Paul considered himself a runner who would not quit until the race was won and he was home with the Lord.

The bottom line is that you must look in the mirror and tell yourself, "I am a minister of the gospel of Jesus Christ and I *must* run the race to completion." Gentlemen, the Church needs you to *run again.* You might be running wounded, but you must run, nevertheless. Get to the starting line—the gun is about to go off and you need to be ready to burst off the starting blocks when it does.

PART ONE:

What you Must Stop Doing

What You Must Stop Doing: Part 1

BLAMING OTHERS

Pastor Tom—or rather *former* Pastor Tom—sat at his computer staring at the spreadsheet. He had worked tirelessly on this project. The shock and numbness of his elders turning on him and firing him during an emergency elder board meeting a month ago had now given way to analysis and waves of grief mixed with anger. Trying to re-create the events leading up to this life-changing meeting, he began entering dates, conversations, emails, and even emotional impressions into this spreadsheet. False accusations, combined with slanted interpretations of the truth, had tainted the judgment of many others until the tide turned unalterably against Tom. It was still astonishing to him that people he had loved, shepherded, and counseled could turn such a cold shoulder to him and to his family. How had it happened? Where did it start?

He believed he had the answer. Tracing the beginning of this effort to get rid of him, he had narrowed it down to two men who had really been the primary instigators. He printed the extensive document, perused it once more, and ran down the hall to find his wife, Gina.

"This is it!" he said excitedly. "I knew I'd find the thread." With a grimace oddly opposite of his supposed joy, he slid the document across the dining room table where Gina was reworking the family finances. Her eyes were sad as she looked first at the multiple pages and then slowly up to her husband.

"What thread?" she asked, knowing she would have to relive the story yet again.

"I can pinpoint exactly when all this started. This was two of the elders, Jack and Howard, all along. They are the ones who turned against me and began a campaign to smear my reputation." His voice was intense and elevated in emotion. He was breathing hard as if the jog down the hallway had been a mile.

Patiently, Gina read the many pages as Tom checked back every 15 seconds to see if she was done. On his final return to the dining room, seeing that she was finished, he looked to her for a positive response. She said two words: "Now what?"

It was like a brick between the eyes. "What do you mean, 'Now what?'" he asked impatiently.

Gina, normally patient and fairly quiet, had a quick flame in her eyes and voice. She stood up, gesturing with emotion.

"What I *mean* is that you were fired a month ago and you've talked about Jack and Howard for hours every day. They are not returning your phone calls or emails; none of the other elders are willing to discuss it with you; the few friends who have stood by us are counseling you to move on—so my question is *really* very simple: *Now what?*"

THE ANATOMY OF BLAME

Tom's wife asked a valid question. For the moment let's operate under the assumption that Tom was literally completely fault-less—that there really was a conspiracy that contained no grain of truth. So we're not talking about blaming others when some of the fault actually lies with Tom. Scripture certainly con-demns blaming others falsely. Proverbs 3:30 warns us to "not contend with a man for no reason, when he has done you no harm." But we'll leave that variable out of the equation for now.

Blaming others is a basic human characteristic since the fall of mankind into sin. Adam defended his sinful action of eating the forbidden fruit by blaming his wife and blaming God for *giving* him his wife (Gen 3:12-13). The people of Israel blamed Moses for the perceived dangers and hardships they faced in the wilder-ness (Num 20:5). When in distress, it seems that it is our sinful instinct to blame others to relieve our own emotional misery.

We might understand blame by thinking in anatomical terms:

- The heart of blame may assign responsibility and fault to others with a perception that you are able to objectively do so. This is the obsession of the heart—to come to conclusions about the core rea-sons you were mistreated or cast aside. Generally speaking, the ultimate conclusion is not often, "I was to blame."

- The ears of blame may selectively hear only what contributes to your established hypothesis. As you speak to others or replay conversations in your mind, those fragments which help your case echo repeatedly while opposing arguments may fade quickly from hearing.

- The eyes of blame may see only what justifies you and lays fault with others. As you recall actions of others, it is possible to construct a panoply of memories that only include harmful actions and do not include the whole of the person or persons being recalled.

- The hands of blame have you doing that which feeds this monster rather than doing the things needed to take care of your family during this time of crisis. Time is wasted building a case never to be heard, writing documents never to be read, or idly focused intently on wrongs never to be righted. Your actions become self-focused.

- The feet of blame may lead to visits to others to plead your case. You may spend time with a supporter or friend replaying and revisiting every nuance and detail—sometimes forgetting that you may be causing another to stumble by wasting inordinate amounts of his time in a fruitless endeavor.

- The mouth of blame may verbally denigrate and put down those you believe responsible for the tragedy you have experienced. Inhibitions are abandoned and all thoughts of sinful gossip or character assassination are replaced with self-aggrandizing rationalizations that "these frauds need to be exposed."

- The mind of blame may think continually negative—even sinfully hateful—thoughts about those
  you find to be at fault. More than one devastated
  pastor has confessed to literal murderous thoughts
  toward those whom he perceived caused harm.

The False Pot of Gold at the End of the Blaming Rainbow

I have asked men this same question after they put forward to me their clear case for being wronged by so-and-so:
"Now what?" The false promise that we tend to tell ourselves is that if we can clearly establish in our own minds the
guilt of others involved in the ministry debacle, *then we will
somehow feel better.* The need for vindication and emotional
relief can become so strong that we lie by telling ourselves
that establishing blame and fault will give us both of those
things. In fact, nothing could be further from the truth.
There is no pot of emotional gold at the end of the blaming
rainbow. I've never once heard a man say, "Now that I've
established in my mind whose fault this really was, I feel
free and happy now."

Instead, when the assigning of fault doesn't satisfy, what was
merely a non-productive waste of time can slip quickly into the
insidious sin of desiring vindictive "justice"—really just a euphemism for *vengeance.* I don't need to quote to you the "vengeance
is mine" Bible verses for you to know the depths of darkness into
which the heart of a vengeful man will sink. But some of the
most wicked and merciless wishes I have ever heard have come
from the lips of the wronged pastor or church leader. *Now* the

blaming has turned the hard corner of wishing ill upon those he blames. This is not just a false pot of gold—it is wicked in the sight of God and considered on par with murder (Matt 5:22).

THREE BLAMING ACTIONS THAT HURT YOU AND OTHERS

Characterizing yourself as a victim. A true victim is someone who can clearly point to themselves as completely innocent and another as completely guilty. A five-year-old child who is abused by an adult family member is clearly the victim and the adult clearly the bad guy. A man injured in a terrorist bombing just because he happened to be walking down the wrong street at the wrong time is clearly the victim. In the case of a ministry catastrophe, it is a lot more difficult to clearly assign this sort of obvious blame.

In the case of Tom, did Jack and Howard have any legitimate complaints that went unheard? Who made them elders in the first place? Were they properly vetted and tested? Did Tom develop relationships with these men such that they would see him not just as the church pastor, but as their friend as well? Did Tom have a history of not receiving correction or suggestion well? Was there any point where Tom could have averted this disaster with a more humble approach to the situation? To characterize yourself as a victim is likely not completely accurate, and again leads us to the question, "Now what?" Even a true victim as described above at some point has to take responsibility for moving forward and not letting the perpetrators take up residence in his life and mind.

Repeating your story continually to help you feel better. I don't deny the legitimate need to seek counsel and to have a couple of safe people to help you walk through this agony. This is vital and helpful. However, the perceived need to tell your story 10,000 times until it doesn't hurt anymore is a concept that has infiltrated our thinking courtesy of secular psychology. I have personally been to counseling seminars where the "expert" taught that to overcome great emotional trauma, the counselee should tell their story repeatedly in the name of desensitization to the pain. And the fact is that despite your best intentions of objectivity, you are still telling the story from your perspective only unless you are making a concerted effort to be brutally honest about your own culpability in the situation. So when you tell the "story," it's not really the whole story. Ultimately, you have to honestly evaluate your motives for telling the story—is it to gain sympathy? To prove a point about how much pain you have endured? At some point, the story is, "God allowed great trials in ministry and He has been faithful at every point before, during, and after." Period.

Underestimating the futility of blame. As mentioned above, the likelihood of blaming others leading you down a road of telling many others your conclusions is astronomically high. In an attempt to minimize the humiliation we feel, we present an air-tight case against the perpetrator of our disaster. In the end, however, the opposite result can happen. Proverbs 11:12 warns us that "whoever belittles his neighbor lacks sense, but a man of understanding keeps silent." The more you put down those you are blaming, the more your listeners may suspect you of sinful bitterness and a shallow faith in the Lord. Practically speaking, you can't really do anything about those you blame for your hurt—but you do have a responsibility to pay attention to your own sanctification through the process. Blaming others is a waste of time in that is doesn't contribute one iota toward your own maturity and sanctification.

A BETTER WAY

If you have stuck it out through the first few pages of this book, you may be thinking, "This guy is punching me in the nose—doesn't he know I need empathy and a soft touch right now?" When I went through an agonizing period in ministry, a time when I felt like I was drowning in dark hopelessness, I had no one to guide me through the murky waters of my own sinful reactions. What I wish someone had done was to jerk me up out of my own self-pity and point my head directly to the face of Christ once again. By God's grace, that happened, but to my shame far too slowly. Perhaps your process can go faster in the following ways.

First, trust God to be judge and focus your words on praise, not blame. The writer of Psalm 71 prays for *God* to judge and vindicate but concerns himself with hoping in the Lord. He writes, "May my accusers be put to shame and consumed; with scorn and disgrace may they be covered who seek my hurt. But I will hope continually and will praise you yet more and more. My mouth will tell of your righteous acts, of your deeds of salvation all the day, for their number is past my knowledge." The lesson is clear: let *God* do the blaming while *you* praise him for His countless blessings.

Second, take Christ as your example. I have repeatedly spoken of, wept through, rejoiced in, and sung out Hebrews 12:3, "Consider him who endured from sinners such hostility against himself, so that you may not grow weary or fainthearted." If I could bluntly state this in the negative: *Every moment you spend blaming others is a moment you are not considering Christ.* Why focus our hearts, minds, and mouths on sinful mortals when we could focus ourselves on the only truly innocent One, Jesus Christ, who silently endured the humiliation of false accusation even to death?

Third, if you truly believe someone has sinned and you have the opportunity to point this out according to Matthew 18:15, *only* do it if you truly know in your heart that this is for *his* benefit, *not* your own. It may be that a significant period of time may need to pass before you are able to do this. It may be that the better part of wisdom is to let the Holy Spirit do the confronting and you just work on humbly looking to Christ. I have personally seen situations where repentance happened even years later simply due to the work of the Spirit in the lives of those who wronged their pastor.

Finally, really believe Romans 8:28. Many of you have likely memorized that "we know that for those who love God all things work together for good, for those who are called according to his purpose." It's one thing to quote the verse; it is quite another to really believe it and have that belief translate into peace and tranquility in your heart. If all things work together for good in God's plan for you, you don't need to supplement His plan with blaming others. Let the disaster work for good—either in this life or in the life to come.

THE OBVIOUS ALTERNATIVE

The only alternative to blaming others is to joyfully acknowledge the sovereignty of God. That will be covered in detail in a different chapter, but I highlight God's sovereignty here because the opposite of trusting God's sovereignty is to blame others. You cannot say, "I trust God's sovereignty," while working feverishly on assigning the right amount of blame to the right people. Either trust God or blame others—the choice is yours.

A Prayer of Humility
before the Eternal God

Eternal Father, I bow on my knees before you first to acknowledge my smallness and your might and greatness. I confess I am plagued by thoughts tempting me to blame others, accuse others, and even hate others. I confess that I have believed I know the whole story, when in reality only You have all the details. Help me to have compassion, love, and hope for those that I perceive have hurt me. Forgive me for thinking that I don't deserve to be hurt. Remind me of Christ who endured such humiliating treatment at the hands of the very men of whom he would pray, "Father, forgive them, for they do not know what they are doing." I am yours to be lifted up or to be crushed. I am yours to be dealt with gently or painfully. The countless blessings you have brought in my life make what little pain I have endured fade into nothing as I contemplate your generosity, most greatly expressed at the cross of Jesus Christ. Teach me to pour out my heart to you before I open my mouth to others. Teach me to be humble before you and to find my rest and safety on my face rather than on my feet. Amen.

DEFENDING YOURSELF

Right on the heels of the previous chapter, the other side of the coin of blaming others is the next logical step in sinful thinking: defending yourself. Now that blame has been established, the case for your own innocence must be established to others, right? Certainly, if the second-worst trial in ministry is being falsely accused, then the top of the list is when others believe the false accusations. To have those to whom you have ministered now look at you with a lessened degree of trust is devastating. And you find yourself in a horrible bind: if you don't defend yourself you look guilty and if you do defend yourself you look selfish.

As I stated in the introduction, this book is primarily for the church leader in the situation where the day has been lost already—the horse is out of the barn and the possibility of recovery is next to non-existent. There is a whole other set of considerations if you are falsely accused and still in the midst of the ministry situation. That is another discussion. What I am focusing upon is dealing with the post-disaster clean-up process.

A Composite Case Study

Meet Jim. Associate Pastor Jim accepted his position in a medium-sized church, applying himself to a variety of ministry responsibilities. The longer he served, the more he saw signs of lack of integrity by the senior pastor and even by some of the elders who were the senior pastor's staunch supporters. He confronted the senior pastor as well as tried to enlist some of the other elders to help. In a classic "good ol' boy" move, rather than pursue righteousness and integrity before the Head of the Church, one Tuesday morning, Pastor Jim was called to the senior pastor's office. He was told to clean out his desk and that this was his last day as associate pastor. Aside from the emotional shock of his sudden dismissal, Jim nearly fell over when the senior pastor told him *questions about Jim's moral purity had been raised.*

"By whom?!" was Jim's natural reply.

"That's not important; it is best to just let this go quietly," the senior pastor said. "The church will pay you for a couple more months so you can get on your feet, but considering the seriousness of this offense, you should feel lucky to be getting that."

Jim asked again through gritted teeth, "Who—is—accusing—me—of—what?" Just then, his cell phone buzzed; it was his wife, Lisa. He took a deep breath and answered. She was crying.

"Felicia just called me," Lisa said between sobs. "She said she would be praying for our marriage 'during this time of trial' and that she believed you would ultimately do the right thing. What was she talking about?"

Jim glared at the senior pastor, then told his wife, "I'll call you right back. I'm coming home right now." He got up and walked to his office, grabbed his car keys, and stormed out of the church. On the way home, he told Lisa what had just happened. Fortunately, she knew that Jim had been concerned about the integrity of the leadership and she did not believe the vague, false accusations. He arrived home and he and Lisa wept together before the kids got home from school.

And just like that, Jim was out. No chance to leave gracefully and untrue rumors left behind to smear his reputation. The urge to defend himself was nearly overwhelming. It was well past midnight when Jim was still at his computer outlining his innocence and all the circumstances that led to his dismissal. He had been physically ill numbers of times throughout the evening and Lisa had barely been able to stay calm in front of the children before they went to bed. Now, he felt his only recourse was to begin what he knew would be the arduous process of regaining his reputation.

Over the course of the next few days phone calls and emails began coming. Most were supportive though in the dark as to the vague accusations, but all had a tinge of belief that Jim had stepped over a moral line since obviously he had been let go by the church. It was agonizing and more than once Jim began to defend himself vehemently. It didn't seem to help but he felt it was his only option.

He began to sense bitterness setting in deeply in his heart and he wanted no part of it. He had seen the destruction that bitterness causes in the lives of believers, so he went to Lisa in humility. "Sweetie, I need your help. I am feeling more and more angry every day and I don't want that. I want to be righteous before God, even in the face of being made to look like a fool."

Lisa held his hand, smiled, and said, "Let's make a battle plan together." And together, they decided that they would no longer try to make a defense, but rather simply assert their love for Christ and one another to any who contacted them. They determined to politely thank people for their concern and to never be rude or curt in response to unwarranted criticism. They even wrote a letter to each individual elder and to the senior pastor genuinely thanking them for every positive thing they could think of, expressing their thanks for the time Jim served with the church. Jim also wrote a polite note to the elders asking them to please let him know precisely who he had offended so that he might make matters right. As he suspected, they ignored his request, confirming in his mind that these were made-up rumors.

THE FAULTY ASSUMPTIONS
OF DEFENDING YOURSELF

Faulty Assumption #1: "I'm defending the church." First Peter 5:2 commands elders to "shepherd the flock of God that is among you." I hate to be blunt, but if you are no longer in a ministry position, then shepherding the flock is not your responsibility. Men I have spoken to who use the phrase, "I'm defending the church," are often using that as a cover for defending *themselves.* Your genuine love and care for the church should be expressed in doing all you can to minimize the continued pain this is causing for others.

Faulty Assumption #2: "I'm defending my good name." I would assert that in actuality you are doing continued damage to what is left of your reputation. Members of the congregation will begin to see you in an even lesser light if you continue on the path of defending yourself. Proverbs 29:11 reminds us that "a fool gives full vent to his spirit, but a wise man quietly holds it back." Perhaps more familiar to us is Proverbs 17:28, that "even a fool who keeps silent is considered wise; when he closes his lips, he is deemed intelligent." Demonstrate your Christ-like character by choosing to end hostilities as quickly as possible.

Faulty Assumption #3: "I'm not causing any harm; I'm just trying to clear my reputation." At the beginning of the process of recovery from disaster, there may certainly be a need to at least state your position (see Appendix C, "Communicating Your Position Without Blame or Aggressive Defense"), but a continued campaign of emails, phone calls, and meetings ultimately serves a very selfish purpose that drains the resources of the ministry. Yes, leaders may need correction and enlightenment, but think of the precious sheep—even the ones who may think less of you now—and do what is right for them. Don't continue disrupting their lives or the shepherding process that is happening in their lives. Every email, phone call, and meeting that you engage in drains energy away from the ministry.

Faulty Assumption #4: "My opponent will have a sudden change of heart once I present my case." It has been well-documented that at the beginning of the American Civil War, soldiers from both sides genuinely thought that the sight of their army marching against the other would provoke a sudden change of mind toward their way of thinking. Many men actually believed that as battle lines were drawn, the other side would simply lay down their arms and come shake hands. As history shows, nothing could be further from the truth. As you defend yourself, in order to allow you to be vindicated, someone else is going to have to admit mistakes or sin. Sinful human nature is such that the likelihood that someone still in power in the ministry will suddenly admit fault is next to none. Frankly, once someone has decided in their heart that you are the bad guy, everything you say will simply make it worse. If you apologize, the apology will be called disingenuous. If you don't, you will be thought unrepentant. Once a person has crossed that line into utter sinful bitterness, there is little you can say that will make it better, and defending yourself will fall on deaf ears. The Lord must be the one to change hearts and He doesn't need your help to do so.

Faulty Assumption #5: "I can give an objective defense." Ministry tragedy, as you know all too well, is an emotionally devastating event. My own ministry trials were far worse emotionally than even when my father was killed in a car accident. If you are trying to make a defense right on the heels on your tragedy, I believe that it would be nearly impossible for you to leave emotion and self-pity out of the defense. One man told me of literally banging the keys of his computer as he constructed his way-too-long defense document. And his anger showed through in his words, yet he didn't see it that way.

What Do I Do Instead?

Remember Jesus Christ. These are the exact words of the apostle Paul to Timothy in 2 Timothy 2:8. What a simple and beautiful admonition, to "remember Jesus Christ." Isaiah 53:7 reminds us that Messiah "opened not his mouth; like a lamb that is led to slaughter." Jesus was the only truly innocent man to ever walk the earth, yet he made no personal defense. Obviously, there was a bigger redemptive plan involved in his case, but his example stands firm for us. Jesus was silent because he had the big picture that God would take care of him *and* take care of those who oppressed him.

Demonstrate Grace. Oh, how tempted you will be to vilify those who have acted like your enemies—to gossip and to have long fiery conversations with your supporters. Instead, take the high road. Take to heart Ephesians 4:29 to "let no corrupting talk come out of your mouths, but only such as is good for building up, as fits the occasion, that it may give grace to those who hear." Be an example to those who are observing your life during this crisis. Let every word from your mouth be uplifting and never denigrating even those who hurt you most. Trust me, you will sleep better.

Let the Lord Vindicate. How many times in the Psalms does the psalmist cry out for vindication from those who oppress him! Vindication is indeed a major sub-theme in Psalms. Psalm 26:1 give the prayer, "Vindicate me, O LORD, for I have walked in my integrity, and I have trusted in the LORD without wavering." But notice a couple of key elements to this prayer. First, the writer is asking the Lord to do the vindicating. Second, the psalmist is keenly aware of his own personal integrity before the Lord. Finally, there is an unshakable nature to his trust: "without wavering." Beware that your so-called defense is not actually a subtle attempt at vengeance of any kind.

Think on God's Timetable. Our emotional distress leads us down the path of desperately seeking vindication and resolution. Sometimes despite your most godly and gracious efforts, people will turn their hearts sinfully against you. Recall that the Lord works in years and centuries and millennia more than he does in hours, days, or weeks. All may be resolved soon, or in five years, or perhaps not until you reach the halls of heaven. Be at peace with God's timetable and rest in his care. God will generally be slower than you wish Him to be.

THE FINAL DEFENSE AGAINST
A DEFENSE: THE GOSPEL

Finally, before getting gung ho about building your case, recall the case that God had built against you. You were dead in your trespasses and sins, a rebel against the Lord shaking your fists in the face of Almighty God. You were guilty as charged. "Yeah, yeah, I know the gospel," you might be tempted to retort. Well, has the gospel put its hands on your cheeks to turn your face once again to the Savior and to remind you of the joy of your salvation? You think you need a defense? How about the ultimate defense that God has made on your behalf already: "There is therefore now no condemnation for those who are in Christ Jesus" (Rom 8:1). You probably have this verse memorized, but read it as if it were the first time. There is *now*—at the present moment—*no condemnation* for you. Whether or not humans have a gripe against you is not the issue. The bigger issue is that the Holy Almighty Sovereign God now *has nothing against you*! Take your eyes off the perceived condemnation of men and turn them instead to the God who has made you clean in His eyes.

Romans 8 goes on to give an impassioned reminder of our privileged status with God. You have received the "Spirit of adoption as sons by whom we cry, 'Abba! Father!'" (v. 15). You know the theology of this verse -- don't miss the emotion of it. This is a child of God coming to grips with the safe, glorious, advantaged, honored position he enjoys in Christ. Paul continues with a verse that should be tattooed to your forehead backwards so you see it every time you look in the mirror, tempted to defend yourself: "For I consider that the sufferings of this present time are not worth comparing with the glory that is to be revealed to us" (v. 18).

You don't need a defense because *you have already been defended*. "Who shall bring any charge against God's elect? It is God who justifies" (v.33). If the Lord sovereignly decreed that you suffer in the ministry, whether self-inflicted or others-inflicted, then you say with Paul, "For your sake we are being killed all the day long; we are regarded as sheep to be slaughtered" (v.36). And of course Paul follows this with the great exclamation of our union with Christ, ending with that fact that nothing "will be able to separate us from the love of God in Christ Jesus our Lord" (v.39).

WHAT YOU MUST STOP DOING: PART 2

A Prayer of Vindication
before the God of Justice

My Just God, please forgive me for any way that I have sought to give justice to myself for the sake of my own satisfaction. You alone are the True Vindicator. You alone will make all things right. For those who have come against me, I pray first that any who are false believers would come to know the true gospel and be saved. Be merciful to them as You have been to me. For those who know You, should they require your loving hand of discipline, I leave that entirely to you. I leave all matters of justice to You. I thank you that I have not received the just punishment for my sin, but instead Christ bore the wrath due me. Remind me that justice is your province, not mine. May the truth of all matters be eventually brought to light, including the truth of how I have not honored You. Shed light on all sin that you might cleanse and forgive all involved. For the sake of Christ, Amen.

WORRYING CONSTANTLY

I can see it like it was yesterday. I was eight years old and in my usual fashion trying to do the job of adults—making sure that details of the summer day planned with my dad and brother were going to go exactly by design. Always concerned with upcoming events, I was literally wrapped in worry about whatever events the day held. My dad sat down with me and said something to the effect of, "Steve, you worry more than your grandmother does. You are a worry-wart." He assured me that he was taking care of the details and that I should just relax and enjoy the day. Although it wasn't until years later that I humorously realized that he was somewhat insulting me, at the time I found it a great relief to "give" the reins back to my dad.

I have battled worry my whole life. I am the master of the worry-session. I can cause myself physical illness, sleepless nights, stomach aches, massive emotional exhaustion—I dare anyone to say they can out-worry me. For me, this is the "sin which clings so closely" (Heb 12:1). I have preached on worry often—as much to be encouraged in my own heart as to encourage others. So when I talk about worry this is not theoretical for me. And when ministry disaster hits you, the plethora of topics about which to fret is like a dark, sinister all-you-can-worry buffet. I don't need to create that list for you; it is already passing through your mind even as you read.

I do not have a cure-all for worry that is devoid of personal effort on your part. What we do have, however, is an amazing passage of Scripture that gives us the path to defeat worry: Philippians 4:4-9. Here we find four weapons with which to attack worry and anxiety. You have to mount an offense and take the battle to the enemy.

FOUR WEAPONS TO ATTACK WORRY

I will devote most of our attention to the final weapon, the nuclear bomb that is the fatal blow to anxiety, but consider the first three weapons a preliminary strike on the enemy of worry.

Weapon #1: Worship the Right God. Philippians 4:4 reminds us to "rejoice in the Lord always; again I will say, rejoice." Worry is wrapped up in a great temptation: the false belief that a certain outcome to your situation is necessary for happiness. When we get wrapped up in *anything* other than our Great God being necessary for happiness, we have essentially set up an idol which we worship. This idol is the belief that only a specific outcome can bring peace and contentment. Now, I am guessing that many of you reading this have preached messages on contentment, likely even from Philippians. Great! Now is the opportunity to put that knowledge into practice. There is no easy way to say this: if you are holding onto the idol of specific outcomes, this is a sin of idolatry that must be forsaken. Your prayer should be, "Lord, I want to rejoice in You and You alone! No situation or outcome or person can make me joyful. You alone are my source of endless peace and joy."

Weapon #2: Exhibit the Right Character. Verse five continues, "Let your reasonableness be known to everyone. The Lord is at hand." *Reasonableness* is speaking of a forebearing spirit. Elsewhere in the New Testament, the English Standard Version translates the same Greek work "gentleness." It is always used in the context of how you behave around other people. The temptation in the midst of great trial such as ministry disaster is to be focused solely on your own feelings. High levels of anxiety impair your ability to care for those around you. Remember, you are still the leader of your family and even though ministry disaster has happened, there are still other saints looking to see how you will handle this adversity. Those around you need you to be joyful, not continually sullen and down. This doesn't mean trying to generate false emotion, but it does mean being sufficiently grounded in the gospel and in the help of the Holy Spirit that you can be an example of fortitude and joy in the midst of pain and grief.

When Jesus' forerunner, friend, and cousin, John the Baptist, was murdered, Matthew chapter 14 records that when Jesus heard this news, he took a boat ride in his grief. When he came to the shore, a huge crowd had gathered. Jesus could have said, "Get away from me! I feel terrible! Leave me alone!" Instead, "he had compassion on them and healed their sick" (v. 14). This was just hours after hearing of John's murder. His concern for others did not diminish even in the face of deep emotional anguish.

Unchecked anxiety leads to sinful behavior. Your wife and children and those closest to you need you to continue in obedience to the Lord rather than allowing a bad situation to control your actions.

Weapon #3: Pray the Right Prayers. Philippians 4:6 continues with a familiar exhortation. "Do not be anxious about anything, but in everything by prayer and supplication with thanksgiving let your requests be made known to God." You and I both know that prayer is essential and no doubt you are praying more than ever, and I praise the Lord for that! However, when faced with disaster, the temptation is to default to emergency 911 prayer mode, jettisoning all types of prayers to simply cry out, "Mayday, Mayday! God, get me out of this situation!" But Philippians 4:6 gives us a better way: Pray with specific goals in mind.

First, take everything to the Lord. And I mean everything. You need to have some prayer sessions in which you take every detail of your situation to the Lord. You cry, weep, groan, explain and specify all aspects of your situation. Be prepared; just one of those prayer sessions might last several hours. How do you know when you are done? When the sense of peace, calm, and resolve is so clear in your own heart that you can rise from your knees with a new smile. "Oh, but you shouldn't pray expecting for an immediate answer." For most issues, I would agree with that statement. However, in this case, we get a direct promise in verse seven: "And the peace of God, which surpasses all understanding, will guard your hearts and your minds in Christ Jesus."

Second, your impassioned requests are to be done in a spirit of thanksgiving. If you are having a problem being thankful, let me start the list for you:

- "Lord, thank You that this trial is driving me to prayer."

- "Thank You that you are sovereign over this situation."

- "...that peace is guaranteed by Philippians 4:7."

- "...that You will make me more like Christ through this."

- "...that your plan in my life is not finished."

- "...that You love me as your son and show it in discipline."

- "...that I have life and breath and continue to enjoy the basic pleasures of daily life."

- "...that I have [insert names of loved ones and family] behind me and in my corner."

- "...that Jesus took the penalty for my sin and I am guaranteed a future heavenly inheritance."

- "...that someday, whether in this life or in the life to come, all will be made clear and your profound wisdom will cause me to worship You all the more."

- "...that I have full and continual access to the throne of grace where I will find help in the time of need."

Weapon #4: Think the Right Thoughts. This is the nuclear bomb to take out worry and anxiety. Verse eight continues with a final command. "Finally, brothers, whatever is true, whatever is honorable, whatever is just, whatever is pure, whatever is lovely, whatever is commendable, if there is any excellence, if there is anything worthy of praise, think about these things." The grammar of this command is clear: the content of your thoughts is something that you control on purpose, obviously through the power of the Spirit of God. It is a disciplined act of the will and mind to specifically guide your thoughts in a biblical direction.

Think on things that are *true.* This speaks of that which is a firm reality, a factually-based thought-life rather than an emotionally-based thought life. In moments of worry, your emotions will lie to you like a little heathen; how you feel is a terrible way to judge anything. Instead, you tell yourself the truth: "God, in His sovereignty, allowed this ministry disaster." "God will take care of me." "I do *not* have to over-react." "My emotions do *not* have to rule me right now." "Even if I *feel* bad, I can still obey the Lord in prayer and worship."

Think on things that are *honorable.* This Greek word is used three other times in the New Testament and always speaks of being "dignified." This word in ancient Greek literature meant to think lofty thoughts—think on things that are majestic, royal, splendid, and noble. Of course, the ultimate in lofty thoughts you can think are focused on the person of God Himself. Rather than cultivating hateful, resentful, and bitter thoughts, are you cultivating glorious, honorable thoughts of Christ? Have you closed your eyes and walked with Him down the road to the cross and revisited Golgotha to see His crucifixion? Have you rejoiced as you see in your mind's eye through the Scripture that glorious moment in the white spaces between Matthew 27 and 28 when Jesus took His first breath of resurrection? Have you marveled at what it must have been like to watch Him ascend into heaven and to hear the promise from the angels that He would return in like manner? These are honorable things, but you *have to think them on purpose.*

Think on things that are *just.* This is often translated in the New Testament as "righteous" or "sincere." These are thoughts that are in conformity to God's standard of righteousness. Am I thinking sinful unholy thoughts about this situation, or am I thinking the thoughts God wants me to think? When Paul was in his first Roman imprisonment, writing the letter to the Philippians, he gave a stunning example of thinking the right thoughts. While he was in prison some were publically proclaiming the gospel *and* insulting the apostle, likely claiming that God was now *against* Paul as demonstrated by his imprisonment. Paul's response is nothing short of just: In Philippians 1:18, he rejoices doubly that Christ is proclaimed, *even if the gospel is going forth by the lips of those who are against him.* This is a just thought.

Think on things that are *pure.* When faced with anxiety, we are often tempted to try to fend off those feelings by numbing our brains with alternative input. These can even be morally neutral things used to excess such as television, internet usage, or other forms of entertainment. Or worse, this alternative input can delve into wicked and sinful areas such as pornography. The admonition is clear: think the pure thoughts of God, thoughts that could be transcribed and read aloud in heaven without shame. Of course, the clearest way to do this is to pour the thoughts of Scripture into your mind. If you haven't tripled your intake of Scripture during this time, you are just setting yourself up to succumb to impure thoughts.

Think on things that are *lovely*. This is the only time this Greek word is used in the New Testament. It speaks of things that are agreeable, kind, friendly, generous, and pleasant. In the Old Testament, the concept of pleasantness is seen often. A great example is found in Psalm 135:3, "Praise the Lord, for the Lord is good; sing to His name, for it is pleasant!" Are your thoughts gracious, sweet, and pleasant? If you could materialize your thoughts into a physical object, would it be something with which to decorate your dining room table, or hide in your tool shed behind the lawn mower?

Think on things that are *commendable*. We get our English word "euphemism" from this word. A euphemism is a substitute word. For example, rather than say "die," we often say, "passed away." The airline industry never officially says than an engine "exploded." Instead, they call it an "uncontained engine failure." We use euphemisms all the time to place a more positive spin on something unpleasant. Paul is calling us essentially to put a positive, godly "spin" on whatever is making us anxious!

- "God will certainly use this situation to help me trust Him more."

- "God's solution will be magnificent."

- "The longer God allows me to wait, the greater the resolution will be."

- "I can hardly wait to see God's glorious purposes for this trial."

The end of verse eight summarizes, "If there is any excellence, if there is anything worthy of praise, think about these things." All in all, in Philippians 4:4-9, there are six commands: (1) rejoice, (2) rejoice, (3) be reasonable, (4) do not be anxious, (5) think on these things and, (6) practice these things. The concluding promise in verse seven is that the peace of God will be yours. In ancient Greek literature, the word for peace spoke of a state of rest or the ability to laugh. True peace will eradicate anxiety and put your laugh back where it belongs—and the circumstances you find yourself in *make no difference whatsoever!* Remember: worship the right God, exhibit the right character, pray the right prayers, and think the right thoughts.

A Prayer of Peace
to the Holy Spirit of Comfort

Holy Spirit, third Person of the Triune God. I may not be used to addressing You directly, but Jesus called You the Comforter and the Counselor. The fruit of the Spirit which you have offered to bear continually in my life includes the fruit of peace. I confess that there are moments or hours or days which are filled with anxiety and concern. I cannot generate peace on my own and I need You, my Helper. I pray for waves of peace and contentment to wash through my heart as I press forward each day trusting the Father to work His perfect will in my life. I pray for my loved ones to have great peace and that I might model for them a joyful, buoyant walk with God. Spirit of God, though You indwell me even now, I ask from the human perspective to give me a clearer sense of your continued presence. I pray for the strength to move forward and that I could look back on this time as one in which I genuinely walked in the peace and security that only You can give. Thank You for testifying in my spirit that I am a child of the living God. Made possible by Jesus Christ, Amen.

SUCCUMBING TO ANGER

"I'm not angry. I'm frustrated," the woman said to her husband emotionally.

"Oh, well that explains how you *frustratedly* just threw your wedding ring in the trash," he retorted back.

And they were off to the races in a usual conflict with each presenting words of righteousness and actions of sinfulness. Life would be much easier if we could check our emotions like checking the oil on the car. If only we could just look at an indicator that said: "Your current mix of emotion is as follows: 25% justified frustration, 25% legitimate grief, 49% sinful anger, and 1% complete murderous rage." Then we would know precisely what is really going on. Because multiple emotions and reactions to trauma and stress happen simultaneously, we have to be extremely discerning about dissecting what is going on. More about that in a moment.

For you who have gone through ministry pain and anguish, it is a particular type of distress that can greatly test your resolve to "walk in a manner of the Lord, fully pleasing to Him" (Col 1:10). I

will use just one example with which all of us are intimately familiar: the replayed conversations. Undoubtedly, a major part of your
trauma has to do with the conversations, emails, or letters that
were exchanged (and may still be) with others in the situation.
People you love and cherish said things to you that were shock-
ing. They may have treated you like an enemy. And now it feels
almost like an obsession to replay those conversations, reread
those emails and letters—only this time you know what you
should have said or how you *should* have replied. It's not unusual
to replay conversations repeatedly and to put a different ending to
them in our minds—an ending where your logic was brilliant and
unstoppable and where your opponent wilted in humble submis-
sion and repentance. And all the while you are feeding the sinful
monster of the belief in your own righteous indignation, which is
nothing more than unrelenting anger in a costume.

Part of dissecting what is happening in your heart is to be
aware of the lies that anger tells us. I don't want to downplay or
underestimate the very real grief involved in the loss you have
experienced, but it's vital to make a distinction. Grief is a natural response to defeat. Anger is a decision you have made. If you
go through the following checklist it should help you put a lid
on sinful anger and give you progress toward moving forward:

LIES ANGER WILL TELL YOU

"You deserve to be angry." The root of this attitude is pride, pure
and simple. Anytime you say you deserve anything whatsoever,
pride is a major player in that drama. By whose standard do you
deserve to be angry? In the mind of the angry person, it is by the

standard that it was precious little *me* which has been hurt. One might even be tempted to say, "This is righteous indignation." We have a wonderful comparison of two situations in which Jesus had a choice about anger. Of course, in His anger He never sinned, but think about this contrast. In situation number one, Jesus (on two different occasions) cleansed the temple of God by turning over money changers' tables and driving the animal sellers out. Clearly, this was righteous indignation. But what was the issue involved? Jesus was defending the good name of *His Father and His Father's house.* In the second situation, when Jesus himself is being accused and tortured, He never displayed anger at all. In fact, He willingly took this abuse ultimately all the way to the cross, asking God to forgive those who were doing this to Him. Certainly, if *anyone* ever deserved to be angry at what was happening to Him, it was Jesus. It is a lie to say that you deserve to be angry. Scripture doesn't support this and the gospel doesn't support this.

"No one understands you." A big part of the need to feel angry is the idea that you are all alone and that no one else could really get what is happening in your heart. I personally wasted significant amounts of time letting this particular thought fester. From a human standpoint, you literally may not know anyone who can really relate to what you have gone through. If that is the case, then it was God's plan for you to walk with Him and Him alone through this. The short answer to the lie "No one understands you" is: *so what?* That doesn't somehow give you the divine right to stay angry with the hope that others will see how angry you are and somehow empathize with you more. That is a fantasy. If no one understands you, then the Lord must be all the more precious to you because *He* certainly

understands. Hebrews 4:15 reminds us that Christ can sympathize with us perfectly, "For we do not have a high priest who is unable to sympathize with our weaknesses, but one who in every respect has been tempted as we are, yet without sin."

"This anger is going to help." Now I know that you don't literally tell yourself that anger will help, but the most insidious of lies are the ones we don't hear directly. If your anger is not going to help, then why are you still angry? Honestly, what do you think will happen positively as a result of your anger? Seriously ponder that question for a moment. I have asked this question of myself when I am angry and of others when they are angry. Most often, the honest answer is that we want attention—we want others to pay attention to us and to express empathy, but our anger has just the opposite effect. On the other hand, God orders you to "let all bitterness and wrath and anger and clamor and slander be put away from you, along with all malice" (Eph 4:31). There is an important distinction to be made. Bitterness, wrath, and anger are all *internal* components of sin. Clamor, slander, and malice are all *external* manifestations of that sin. Clamor is to make trouble. Slander is to hurt someone with words. Malice is to make trouble with the intent to hurt. Anger will ultimately have no positive outcome and in fact will lead you to sin. In Psalm 37, God gives a clear command and the consequences of disobedience, "Refrain from anger, and forsake wrath! Fret not yourself; it tends only to evil." More than one wife of a shattered shepherd has begged her husband to stop being so angry. It comes out in your words, your actions, your facial expressions. It will hurt you and those you love because your anger will cause pain to you and to those you love.

"I can't help being angry." Say this five times aloud to yourself in the mirror. It is my hope that you look and feel like a total wimp by the time you are done. This is the statement of a pathetic victim, not a child of the living God in whom the Holy Spirit resides. The preacher of Ecclesiastes reminds us, "Be not quick in your spirit to become angry, for anger lodges in the heart of fools" (Eccl 7:9). To say you can't help being angry is to completely deny the power of the Holy Spirit to produce the promised fruit of love, joy, peace, patience, kindness, goodness, faithfulness, gentleness, and self-control (Gal 5:22-23). Perhaps you feel the emotion of anger in response to what has happened to you. According to Scripture, however, what you do with that is entirely your call.

The Truth about Anger

Your anger is stopping your sanctification. We are all familiar with James 1:19-20, "Know this, my beloved brothers: let every person be quick to hear, slow to speak, slow to anger; for the anger of man does not produce the righteousness of God." What we don't always remember is the context. James is writing in James 1:19-27 about a godly response to hearing God's Word. This passage warns the listener not to be angry with what they hear from God's Word—that a negative response to the truth will not produce righteousness. You are hearing God's Word explained right now in this text, and the admonition is clear: to rid yourself of leftover anger from your ministry situation. To not do so is to simply stop the process of sanctification that the Lord has planned for you.

Anger is a focus on yourself. Psalm 37:7 makes the distinction that anger is a focus on yourself and that the solution is to wait upon the Lord instead, "Be still before the LORD and wait patiently for him; fret not yourself over the one who prospers in his way, over the man who carries out evil devices!" If you need to, confess the sin of focusing on your own feelings and instead breathe the delightful fresh air of focusing on the Lord and His sovereign care.

Anger is a decision to not trust the Lord. Oh, I know this sounds harsh. Perhaps you are arguing with this book right now in your mind. Before you angrily throw it in your fireplace, ask yourself a question, "If my trust in the Lord was literally perfect, at a scale only found in heaven, how angry would I truly be?" You and I both know the answer. Not only would you not be angry, but your joy in the Lord would be overflowing. Your times of prayer would be filled with sweet tears of delight. Your times in the Word would be nourishing and life-giving. Your demeanor with your loved ones would be pleasant and inspiring. Why? "You keep him in perfect peace whose mind is stayed on you, because he trusts in you" (Isa 26:3).

THE SOLUTION TO ANGER

In my days of deepest pain, when I wrestled with my own disappointment, grief—and yes, deep anger—I could hardly even comprehend what I was reading in Scripture. So I narrowed it down. I decided to camp out in Psalm 63:1-8 and I wasn't leaving it until I was okay again. I spent time in Psalm 63 daily for a couple of months. I wept through it, prayed through it, confessed sin through it, and praised God through it. This beloved text gave me a series of resolutions that drew me out of the pit of despair.

- I must seek God. "O God, you are my God; earnestly I seek you; my soul thirsts for you; my flesh faints for you, as in a dry and weary land where there is no water."

- I must focus on God's glory. "So I have looked upon you in the sanctuary, beholding your power and glory."

- I must praise God. "Because your steadfast love is better than life, my lips will praise you. So I will bless you as long as I live; in your name I will lift up my hands."

- I must be satisfied in God alone. "My soul will be satisfied as with fat and rich food, and my mouth will praise you with joyful lips."

- I must meditate continually on God. "When I remember you upon my bed, and meditate on you in the watches of the night."

- I must remember God's faithfulness. "For you have been my help, and in the shadow of your wings I will sing for joy."

- I must cling to God. "My soul clings to you; your right hand upholds me."

Whatever vestiges of anger you may be hanging onto, whether daily rage or insidious remnants, take it to the throne of grace and leave it there. Let it go, saint.

A Prayer for Self Control
to the God who Controls All

My Lord and King, when Jesus was on earth He faced persecution, torture, and death—all without uttering a word of anger or revenge against His attackers. I am your child; I have the Spirit of Christ within me. Give me the strength to demonstrate the self-control of my Savior. I confess to You the sin of selfish anger and the destruction it has caused my own heart and maybe to those around me as well. I confess to You my trust in you has been inadequate. This day, I leave anger behind and ask You to replace it with the deep satisfaction of the joy of my salvation. You have been my help and in the shadow of your wings I will sing for joy. My soul clings to You because your right hand upholds me. In Jesus' Name, Amen.

VIEWING YOURSELF AS THE TRAGIC HERO

In the famous opening line of Charles Dickens' *David Copperfield,* David states, "Whether I shall turn out to be the hero of my own life, or whether that station will be held by anybody else, these pages must show." David's life is chronicled from his birth to the continual tragedies of his childhood and adult life. Finally, the reader reaches the conclusion that David Copperfield, through a happy ending by way of marriage to the true love of his life, *is*, in fact, the hero of his own life.

Pacing back and forth in his friend's living room, telling his story with gusto and emotion, a recently-fired pastor recounted all the wrongs done against him with all the passion of a Shakespearean actor. His long-honed skill in preaching was bleeding out in his zealous portrayal of how *right* he was and how *wrong* his elders had been. Words like "conspiracy" and "scheme" and "plot" peppered the intense soliloquy. Soon, even his friend was buying into the display, telling his former pastor that he was a "hero of the faith" and that he was, indeed, a victim of terrible cruelty.

Anyone who has been in or around ministry long enough knows that schemes and plots can and sometimes do exist in the church. Since the days of Diotrophes, "who likes to put himself first" (3 John 9), the hunger for power in the church has been a thorn in the side of faithful pastors. But the point is not who was right and who was wrong. The point for the jilted pastor or church leader is to respond in a way that is pleasing to Christ.

There are three problems with the bruised pastor or leader viewing himself as the tragic hero of the story. This view does nothing to heal the inflicted wounds; it elevates self in a destructively sinful manner, and it creates a view of oneself which leads to self-imposed isolation. The "hero-ification" of oneself is a faulty mechanism, a flawed comparison, and a foolish path.

A FAULTY MECHANISM

I know that for many of you reading this, the ministry disaster and pain you have experienced (or may still be experiencing) has caused emotional anguish that can rightly be compared to grief over the death of a loved one. You may have been attacked and maligned by people you love and shepherd. Perhaps you saw trouble brewing and with a sense of helpless foreboding watched as those you thought to be loyal to you and your ministry began trying to systematically destroy the fruit of your labors. You watched as your family suffered along with you, your wife and children seeing the darkness creeping over you week by week.

There is often a deep and desperate desire to have relief from the emotional weight. One of the faulty mechanisms that is so tempting to utilize in order to give some emotional relief is to create a false, overly simplistic dichotomy that says, "I am the good guy and those who did this to me are the bad guys." This downward spiral will begin to blind you to any responsibility you may personally bear and now you can confidently assert that all these horrible emotions are *someone else's fault.* And if they are all someone else's fault, the characterization of yourself as a tragic, persecuted hero *feels like* it will give you emotional relief. Now, you may in fact *be* a tragic, persecuted hero—but it is imperative that you let *the Lord* make that determination and not yourself.

Heman, the author of Psalm 88, cried out to God in despair. Often called the saddest Psalm, Psalm 88 recounts the desperate condition that Heman faced. What was likely some sort of horrible physical illness had caused great suffering on multiple fronts for Heman. He was physically afflicted. He was disoriented in regard to *why* he was having to endure this trial. He was isolated from all who loved him, perhaps because of quarantine-like measures. In fact, Psalm 88, unlike most Psalms of supplication, does not end with the characteristic faithful optimism in the Lord. It seems to end in hopelessness.

But, like many treasures which are buried in the darkness, Psalm 88 reveals that Heman did *not* succumb to the temptation to make himself the hero of his own drama. One of his major areas of suffering was the isolation he endured—he was kept away from all who loved him and was possibly rejected because of this illness. Perhaps he suffered from leprosy which would isolate him from society according to the Law of Moses.

Despite the fact that he felt alone and rejected, he showed that he believed God to be the sovereign cause. He said to the Lord, "You have put me in the depths of the pit" (verse 6); "Your wrath lies heavy upon me" (verse 7); "You have caused my companions to shun me" (verse 8); "Your dreadful assaults destroy me" (verse 16).

There is no mistaking the emotional anguish that has buried Heman in this torturous time—but he never once characterized himself heroically. Certainly he had many questions for the Lord, but his conclusion was clear: this is a test that will be between him and his God. The other people involved were merely tools in God's hands. And from the shadows of despair, Heman points you and me in the right direction. He begins the Psalm, "O LORD, God of my salvation, I cry out day and night *before you.*" Near the end of his plea, he reiterates, "But I, O LORD, *cry to you*; in the morning my prayer comes *before you*" (verse 13, emphasis added).

To paint yourself as the innocent hero, even if it is true, is to run in the opposite direction of where you should be headed. It is a faulty mechanism that will not work or help you. Heman never once asserts his innocence or that he did not deserve this trial. He simply cried out to the Lord for mercy and asked the Lord to glorify Himself through his life (verses 10-12). The focus of Psalm 88 is a laser-beam toward God Himself. Ironically, we are never told whether or not God answered Heman's prayers. But we do know that rather than wrestling with the perceived evil of other men in self-exaltation, he wrestled in prayer with the God who loved Him and did so in self-deprecation.

A Flawed Comparison

In my experience with others and my own personal trials in ministry it is a natural part of viewing yourself as the tragic hero to compare yourself to other *actual* heroes. We think of Jonathan Edwards who was ousted from his ministry of over 20 years. We think of the reformers who often preached at great personal risk. And certainly, more than one suffering pastor has drawn comfort from the apostle Paul's account of his own ministry suffering recounted in 2 Corinthians 11. There seems to be a comfort drawn from placing yourself in the category of great suffering pastors. The problem is that this is a flawed comparison. It can be based on the parts of your story and the parts of the stories of others that you want to acknowledge while not thinking of the whole picture.

Second Corinthians 11 records Paul's recollections of the suffering he had endured in the ministry. He was beaten, flogged, stoned nearly to death, and shipwrecked—*three times*. He was endangered from countless sources. He knew sleeplessness, hunger, cold, heat, and anxiety on behalf of all the churches to which he ministered. Paul's reason for enumerating this suffering to the Corinthian church is tied to one of the purposes of 2 Corinthians: the defense of his apostleship.

One of his defenses was the fact that he had suffered greatly as Jesus had promised apostles in general (Matt 10:16-25) and Paul in particular (Acts 9:15-16). The Corinthian church had apparently mistreated Paul and had caused him great sorrow to the point that he had to reassert his ministry as an apostle. And this is where many hurt men in ministry stop in the story and compare themselves to Paul, even using it as an excuse to continually defend themselves as a self-proclaimed hero. Ministry does cause suffering; anyone in ministry understands this. But that is as far as the comparison can and should go.

First, Paul was not trying to gain sympathy as a hero. Rather, he was defending his apostleship because he cared deeply for the Corinthian church and did not want them to be deceived by false apostles. Second, if you read the context of the entire section of 2 Corinthians 11, you find that it is with humble reluctance that Paul shares his own trials in ministry. His sharing is for the greater purpose of edifying the Corinthians, not for the sinful purpose of exalting himself as a hero. Finally, though Paul could easily and rightfully attribute some of his suffering to the Corinthians themselves, he believed even his suffering to be for their sake, "If we are afflicted, it is for your comfort and salvation" (2 Cor 1:6).

In fact, the final blow to the sinful tendency to view oneself as a tragic hero comes in 2 Corinthians 12:10 when Paul asserts, "For the sake of Christ, then, I am content with weaknesses, insults, hardships, persecutions, and calamities. For when I am weak, then I am strong." Instead of being the self-exalting tragic hero, Paul says that he is *content* (*eudokeo*), which means to take pleasure and be glad! He proclaims his weakness, not as a hero, but as a humble servant of Christ who has found contentment in whatever suffering he endures. No pacing; no Shakespearean proclamation of his innocence; just a meek declaration of his satisfaction with suffering.

To proclaim yourself as a tragic hero just like Paul simply does not hold water. But if you make a choice to humbly receive whatever the Lord brings and see it all as part of God's providential working in your life, then the comparison to the apostle is a worthy one.

A Foolish Path

I have sat with men who have experienced great calamity in ministry, having been attacked in vicious ways in their own church or ministry. On more than one occasion, I have seen a somewhat chilling nuance in their response: a characterization of themselves as different from others, possessing a completely unique calling—a gallant man tragically brought down by the evil empire of the church deacons. While great fault may indeed lie with those who came after them, the chilling part is the description of themselves as *different* and *special*. In an almost prophet-of-God sense, the suffering shepherd can go down the foolish path of separation.

This separation can begin to take many destructive forms. He may begin to withdraw from praying with others. He may begin to become overly introspective to the point of torturing himself with his own thoughts. He may begin to isolate himself emotionally from those closest to him, and that because of the pain he is feeling he must pull within himself as the wounded warrior of God. Others are to walk around him in hushed whispers, quietly praising with awe this hero who has taken so much anguish for the glory of God.

This may seem overly dramatic, but that is precisely the point. Words and phrases like "unique calling," "gallant," and "wounded warrior" have all been used in my presence by men who deal with their emotional pain by seeing themselves as the unique hero of the faith. But the Scriptures tell a different story. Proverbs 18:1 bluntly tells us, "Whoever isolates himself seeks his own desire; he breaks out against all sound judgment."

This is a foolish path because this view of oneself as special in ministry is in direct contradiction to Scripture. Paul—arguably the most effective pastor and missionary in the history of the church—viewed his ministry as "the mercy of God" (2 Cor 4:1). He understood the great privilege of being a minister of the gospel and certainly did not see himself as an irreplaceable piece of the church's overall progress.

It is a subtle and dark wave of self-aggrandizement that leads the wounded pastor or leader to view himself more highly than he ought. This is a path full of mirrors in which you become obsessed with yourself, your feelings, your pride, and your sense of noble martyrdom. If an honest evaluation tells you that this is the path you have taken, shatter the mirrors that reflect the tragic hero back to you and focus instead on the real hero of your story: The Lord Jesus Himself.

STOP VIEWING YOURSELF AND START VIEWING THE LORD

How many sermons or Bible lessons you taught have included an inspired exhortation to look to Jesus, "the Author and Finisher of our faith?" (Heb 12:2). No doubt you have been used of the Lord to bolster the trembling faith of others as they face the inevitable trials of life. When you consider the next few phrases of that Hebrews passage, you are reminded that Jesus endured the cross, withstood the shame, and braved the hostility of sinners so that He might faithfully finish the work of salvation on your behalf.

For a moment, forget the disappointment, the anguish—forget the faces of those you believe have so deeply wronged you. Stop and go back to the cross. Look up at the face of Christ—a face tortured with the agony of bearing your sin, yet filled with deep love for you. Look at the blood flowing down the splintered edges of the cross. Look at the growing darkness around you when Christ will receive the full fury of the wrath of God so that you can leap for joy in the heavenly kingdom someday.

Christ is the true and only hero in the story of your life. If He could endure the cross, then certainly you can take up your cross to follow Him (Mark 8:34). Your cross is to die to self, to be crucified with Christ. You no longer live—Christ lives in you. Take yourself off the pedestal of the immortalized tragic hero and return once again to "a sincere and pure devotion to Christ" (2 Cor 11:3). When Christ is the real hero in your heart once again, peace returns and joy abounds.

A Prayer of Devotion to Christ

Almighty God, in the midst of my own struggles, it is possible that I have elevated myself and my own importance far into the realm of pride. Forgive me if I have viewed myself as anything more than a slave of Christ, redeemed by His precious blood. Convict me of my moments of self-exaltation when I am tempted to campaign for the pity of others. Return my heart to the glory of the gospel, the joy of my salvation, and the certain hope of future glory. This day let my thoughts be drawn continually to Christ, borne along by the power of the Spirit, that all glory may come to You, my Father. For Jesus' sake, Amen.

PART TWO:

What you Must Start Doing

GENUINELY TRUST THE SOVEREIGNTY OF GOD

(The Chapter You're Tempted to Skip)

For most, if not all, of you reading this, this is the chapter you are tempted to skip over: The doctrine of the sovereignty of God—"God is still on the throne—yeah, yeah, I get that." You may be tempted to skip this because you don't need to be intellectually convinced of God's sovereignty. You have no problem believing in the overarching plan of God for history, for the fulfillment of prophecy in Scripture, and for the culmination of His redemptive plan for mankind. However, the trial you have recently endured—or are still enduring—is a wonderful test of how genuinely you trust the sovereignty of God for something smaller, like your life. The key word here is *genuinely* trust.

"Genuine" speaks of being sincere, actual, real, or authentic. When thinking of a belief system, we could extrapolate this to mean something that is truly accepted at the deepest heart level. So to *genuinely* trust the sovereignty of God means that your understanding of God's sovereignty is the deep-seated foundation of your entire response to ministry disaster. It can often take some time for that genuineness to finally materialize in a meaningful way.

I'm reminded of a church member I was counseling concerning a particular trial. I did my best to be empathetic, understanding, and caring. When I thought the time was right, I tried to tenderly bring up the sovereignty of God. Before half a sentence was out of my mouth, the counselee rolled his eyes and said, "*Please* don't quote Romans 8:28 at me." For this person, the intellectual belief in the sovereignty of God had not yet made a difference in his handling of his crisis. To a certain degree, we understand this. When tragedy first strikes, emotion and grief are the overriding experiences. At some point, however, our theology has to gain traction and begin to win the day. And the sooner, the better.

A TINY BIT OF THEOLOGY

Space does not permit an extended doctrinal discussion of divine sovereignty. That is not what you need right now anyway. But we do want to establish a basic foundation, so I will shamelessly expose my Calvinistic leanings with the following definition by John Feinberg: God's sovereignty is . . .

> God's power of absolute self-determination . . . [which] means, of course, that God is the ultimate, final, and complete authority over everything and everyone. Whatever happens stems from his decisions and control. God's sovereign will is also free, for nobody forces

him to do anything, and whatever he does is in accord with his own purposes and wishes.[1]

We are not trying to answer the theological tension between divine sovereignty and human responsibility. I address the human responsibility part in numerous other chapters. Nor are we trying to address the oft-named "problem of evil." We simply want to (a) acknowledge that God is sovereign and (b) explore how this belief works itself out in a response to ministry disaster.

EXAMPLES OF GENUINE TRUST IN THE SOVEREIGNTY OF GOD

Job—While we know that Job had issues which God dealt with later in Job's time of suffering, Job's first response was to acknowledge the sovereignty of God. After hearing news of the loss of family and property, Job said, "Naked I came from my mother's womb, and naked shall I return. The Lord gave, and the Lord has taken away; blessed be the name of the LORD" (Job 1:21). Significantly, the author of Job adds in the next verse, "In all this Job did not sin or charge God with wrong." Job recognized God's total right to do as He pleases. There was no questioning, no anger, and no indignation— just trust in God's sovereignty.

David—When David sinned against the Lord with Bathsheba and God decreed that the child born to them would die, David

---

1 John S. Feinberg, *No One Like Him: The Doctrine of God* (Wheaton: Crossway Books, 2001), 294.

"sought God on behalf of the child" (2 Sam 12:16). He fasted, wept, and lay down all night on the ground seeking God's help. When the baby finally died, David's servants were astonished at his response. He stopped weeping, cleaned himself up, and went to the house of the Lord to worship God. Then he came home and asked for food. His explanation to his surprised servants was that "while the child was still alive, I fasted and wept, for I said, 'Who knows whether the LORD will be gracious to me, that the child may live?' But now he is dead. Why should I fast? Can I bring him back again? I shall go to him, but he will not return to me" (2 Sam 12:22-23). Certainly David's emotions were still raw and grief was upon him, but his foundational understanding of God's sovereignty carried the day. He accepted the will of the Lord and demonstrated this with his actions.

Jeremiah—The book of Lamentations is a set of five poems of sorrow concerning the destruction of Jerusalem in 586 BC. Jeremiah begins poignantly, "How lonely sits the city that was full of people!" (Lam 1:1). You are probably already quoting the most famous verses from Lamentations—"The steadfast love of the Lord never ceases . . . great is your faithfulness" (3:22-23). There is more gold in this mine, however, concerning the sovereignty of God. Just a few verses later, Jeremiah makes a statement about God that is nothing short of amazing. "Who has spoken and it came to pass, unless the Lord has commanded it? Is it not from the mouth of the Most High that good and bad come?" (Lam 3:37-38). There have been attempts to explain away the "bad" part on the basis of God not being able to look upon evil (Hab 1:13). Certainly we affirm the holiness, purity, and sinlessness of God. The problem with trying to explain away the "bad," however, is that verse 37 already qualifies verse 38: that *everything* that happens comes from the Lord. I believe that this understanding was the theological underpinning for Jeremiah to be able to be able to say, "great is your faithfulness." The entire book of Lamentations reads as a lesson in a deeply-rooted knowledge of God's total control in the midst of grief and sorrow.

So, if you want to genuinely trust in the sovereignty of God, I suggest four logical implications that should translate into you sleeping better tonight—if you take them to heart to *genuinely* believe them.

It's Not All about You

In the midst of my own ministry challenges, I couldn't help thinking about four different people continually: yours truly, me, myself, and I. I don't mean just focusing on my own feelings. Rather, as I thought about how God was working mysteriously in my life, my thoughts of God's sovereignty were fixed entirely on *me*. "God is sovereign over *my situation* . . . God is able to bring *me* through this . . . God is dealing incomprehensibly with *me*." Even in the midst of learning about and trying to trust in God's sovereignty, it was still a tunnel vision view.

The powerful truth, however, is that God sovereignly working in your life through pain and anguish has infinitely more far-reaching implications for His total plan. The old default explanation of course is that God allowed you to go through such-and-such so that you could be able to help others later.

There is certainly truth to this, but this explanation leaves a lot to be desired. I like this statement better: "God ordained this trial—not just as a work in my own life—but as part of his overarching plan for the lives of those whom I know, the lives of those whom I know know, the lives of those whom I know know know, etc.

Let's take all variables of blame and fault out. Operating under the assumption that you were perfectly and totally innocent in the ministry disaster which befell you, it is a verifiable fact from Scripture that even a totally innocent episode of suffering could be completely about *someone else besides you.* When Joseph's brothers sold him into slavery, radically altering his life leading to bondage, prison, then even eventual exaltation, he was able to completely forgive his brothers. His reason was based on the fact that God had a bigger purpose: to ultimately save his family and all of Egypt in the midst of a famine. That's why he said to his brothers, "As for you, you meant evil against me, but God meant it for good, to bring it about that many people should be kept alive, as they are today" (Gen 50:20). And the even bigger picture is that this is how God got Jacob's family to Egypt where they would thrive and eventually be enslaved, fulfilling God's prophecy to Abraham in Genesis 15:13-14.

SOVEREIGNTY GIVES PEACE

The Apostle Paul makes the classic statement in Galatians 2:20, "I have been crucified with Christ." In context, he is speaking about the fact that when Christ was crucified, we were credited as having all our sin paid for as if we ourselves had been crucified. And the result is that it "is no longer I who live, but Christ who lives in me." While the implications for the doctrine of justification are clear here, let's get very practical with this. Paul is speaking of the life we live as those crucified with Christ. If I am crucified, dead to myself that "I might live to God" (Gal 2:19), then God's sovereignty tells me that whatever happens to me is okay. If part of living as one crucified with Christ means taking it on the chin in ministry, it doesn't matter—I'm crucified. If it means suffering under the weight of false accusation and character assassination in ministry, it doesn't matter—I'm crucified. There is a real joy to letting this truth sink into your soul. You belong completely to the Lord and you are *his* tool to use *his* way for *his* glory. Your involuntary response to this will be to worship God who gives peace in the eye of the storm.

When Jeremiah wrote the astonishing statement that everything that happens comes from the Lord (Lam 3:37), he gave us an amazing boost in our ability to have peace. *All* that happened to you came straight from the O.O.H.O.—Office of Heavenly Orders. This is cause for tremendous comfort and peace! Let me illustrate: If a child is on his hands and knees cleaning up a mess that someone else made, it makes a huge difference to know whether the child is doing this because a stranger has entered the home and is pointing a gun, or if the child's mother is lovingly teaching a hard lesson about serving others.

If God has not sovereignly directed every single event in your anguish, then you have no basis for peace. If, however, for reasons unknown or known, God is the Divine Architect of your disaster, you can rest easily in the wisdom of His overarching plan.

CHRIST IS THE HEAD OF THE CHURCH

The feeling that you should not have been treated in a certain way is certainly natural, and from a purely human standpoint has merit. But the following fictional story illustrates a sovereignty-of-God vantage point:

> He didn't want to resign, but all the indications were there. So rather than waiting to get fired, Pastor Jack pulled the plug himself. In talking to another pastor, Martin, Jack said with gritted teeth, "I should still be in my pulpit."
>
> With loving directness, Martin replied, "Apparently, Christ doesn't think so. If he wanted you there, you'd still be there. He is the Head of the Church and directs as He pleases. And by the way, it was never 'your pulpit,' Jack. It was always His."

We already know Christ has guaranteed to build His Church from Matthew 16, and we would all agree theoretically that Christ is the Head of the Church—that He is in charge and we submit to his will as revealed in the Scriptures. But consider this: every day of the year somewhere in the world seemingly terrible things are happening to leaders in the Church. Pastors are fired; elders wrongfully removed; unqualified pastors and elders are installed; whole churches fall apart; treasurers steal money. This doesn't even get into the problem of false teaching entering the Church. When you look globally like this, pessimism can be an understandable reaction. But if Christ is *truly* the sovereign Head of the Church, then *all* these things are working together to fulfill He all-encompassing supreme plan.

In John 21, Jesus told Peter "when you are old, you will stretch out your hands, and another will dress you and carry you where you do not want to go" (v. 19). Jesus was telling Peter that he would die a painful death to God's glory. Immediately following this, after seeing John, Peter asked Jesus, "Lord, what about this man?" Peter wanted to know if John was going to get the same sort of deal! As the Head of the Church, Jesus made a definitive statement of complete authority. He told Peter, "If it is my will that he remain until I come, what is that to you? You follow me!" (v. 22). Jesus essentially ordered Peter to not worry about the big picture—that was Jesus' job. Peter's job was "you follow Me!"

The implication is evident: If Christ is the Head of the Church, then whatever happened to you in ministry was part of His total package deal. A general doesn't obligate himself to give explanation of every tactical move and realignment of resources he makes. Neither is Christ obligated to bring you into His "office" and explain how you fit into the big picture. There is great joy in this because you are reminded that you *are*, in fact, part of His dealings with the Church. Your current role is painful and hard, but is part of Christ's plan nonetheless. It is your turn right now to take one for the team and to focus intently on being faithful today, even if this means faithfully enduring a season of grief.

A Retrospective Perspective

I have heard it said that in retrospect, we can see the Lord's wisdom in our trials and even some benefits. Usually, when I hear that, it is with a somewhat resigned "making lemonade out of lemons" tone and attitude. I want go radically beyond this. Let's move farther along in your life. Or if God's wisdom doesn't necessarily manifest itself that soon, then let's move into eternity. Now, turn around and look with the eyes of one who can see all the goodness that came to you personally and how your trial has rippling impacts in countless other lives. Given that perspective, I want to make a radical statement: *God's wisdom is so magnificent and His purposes so glorious that given the opportunity, knowing what you know now, you would gladly go through the same exact trial all over again.* That's the type of perspective you need to have *now*, albeit by faith.

Genuine trust in the sovereignty of God translates into peace, better sleep, and even an excitement about the future that you may have forgotten.

A Prayer of Trust in Our Sovereign Lord

Sovereign Lord, all the workings of my life are firmly in your hands. Your hands are strong and purposeful, and what may feel like the pain of a tight grip is actually the security of a firm hold. You are all-powerful, able to bring about every one of your perfect intentions. And I am no exception. I trust that You are working in my life for my good, the good of my family, the honor of the Church, and the glory of Christ. Break my heart once again to be fully dependent on You, trusting fully and genuinely in Your perfect plan. Remind me that "in peace I will both lie down and sleep; for You alone, O LORD, make me dwell in safety."

ACCEPT THE LOVING DISCIPLINE OF THE LORD

The phone call from Mrs. Harper was encouraging. Leave it to an older saint to have a seasoned response to a crisis. Pastor Dan kept listening to her warm words of reassurance reminding him of Romans 8:28 and God's faithfulness to him. One small difficulty with a church leader had quickly grown into an out-of-control disaster. Leaders took sides and there was just enough gossip to poison the whole church with what should have been a one-conversation cure. Before Dan knew what had hit him, the elders were subtly suggesting that his resignation was the only viable alternative. They left him hung out to dry all by himself. It had only been three weeks since Dan had numbly turned in his resignation and it was still all he could think about, day and night.

Mrs. Harper—always the light of the room—was a rare jewel of joy in this time of anguish for Dan and his family. She continued to speak of the Lord's timing and hope for the future, encouraging Dan to keep his head high and trust the Lord. His wife and children were devastated. They had been in this church for almost a dozen years; they'd raised their children in this church. The church was their life, their social community, their spiritual strength—and now they were alone. Mrs. Harper understood this.

Dan had endured many uncomfortable conversations in the past 21 days, but Mrs. Harper was a drink of water in the desert—or so he thought. Just as she was wrapping up, she threw in one last comment that sent a sword through Dan's heart.

"Well, Pastor Dan, I know the Lord will be faithful to you. I'm sure He is disciplining you for some reason, but the chastening of the Lord doesn't last long and He is very forgiving."

"The discipline of the Lord?" thought Dan. *"I have one small disagreement with a leader in the church, and the Lord would take away my ministry for that? I'm not aware of hidden sin or immorality either. How could she say that?"*

Dan was crushed and slumped into a chair, all the air of Mrs. Harper's encouraging words let out by the final cutting comment.

THE MYTH ABOUT GOD'S DISCIPLINE

Let's just say it: I already know that your situation is due to the discipline of the Lord. Yes, you have been disciplined by God. How do I know this? Because you are His child and He loves you more than you can possibly fathom. The myth about God's discipline is that He only disciplines the disobedient, unruly believers in desperate need of a divine spanking. Yet this is clearly not what Scripture teaches us.

First, God disciplines every single one of His children. In John 15:2, Jesus says that "every branch that does bear fruit, he prunes, that it may bear more fruit." Every believer in Christ bears some spiritual fruit at some level. Since every believer possesses the Spirit of God (Rom 8:9) then the Spirit is active in the life of that person (Gal. 5:22-23). The one who bears fruit—every believer—will be occasionally pruned. Near where we live, there are miles and miles of rolling hills with beautiful vineyards. It forms a scene right out of our imagination about heaven. The grapevines grow lush, green and breathtaking in scope. But every year, these vineyards suddenly look like a nuclear bomb hit them. Every vine has been trimmed back such that all you can see is the basic brown nub of each grapevine. If I were one of those trimmed grapevines, I would be quite embarrassed and hope that someone would cover me until I could grow some leaves again. The owner of the vineyard did not just trim back the vines with which he was unhappy; he trimmed them *all* back so that the following season they might produce all the more fruit. God trims back all his vines to make us more effective for Him.

Second, God disciplines out of love. Hebrews 12:6 reminds us that "the Lord disciplines the one He loves, and chastises every son whom He receives." In fact, the writer of Hebrews goes on to say that if God does *not* discipline you, you are not his child (v.8). A right understanding of the Lord's discipline is that (a) this comes to all believers, (b) it is done out of love for me, (c) and it is that which will help me become more like Christ (Rom 8:29). I know this may sound a little extreme, but if God's discipline proves the genuineness of your faith, demonstrates His love for you, and propels you toward Christ-likeness, our attitude toward discipline should be to *desire it deeply*, not resent it or wish it would go away!

Cause-Effect or Just God's Sovereign Timing?

The Lord's faithful chastising may be a little harder to swallow when you cannot see a direct cause-effect relationship. We like to be very black and white. Take, for example, the man who is running around on his wife despite warnings from his brothers in Christ: when he is in a car accident that leaves him in the hospital for a month, we think to ourselves, *"Well, that's an open-shut case of God's discipline."* But what about your situation where it is likely you were blindsided, caught completely off-guard and suddenly in pain for no apparent reason? Now the waters get more murky when trying to establish cause-effect. If it were always obvious cause-effect, we would not see outstanding men of the Word in ministry suffering for the Savior while men who should never have been in church leadership seem to thrive no matter how incompetent or unbiblical they may be as shepherds. Clearly, we rest simply on the sovereignty of God's timing. But what *do* you do with the whole discipline issue?

Take Advantage of an Opportunity

It does no good to deny that the Lord's loving hand of discipline is at work. So now that we've established that discipline is a player in this drama, we can settle in to make discipline work on our behalf. In his commentary on the book of Hebrews, Thomas Lea gives the following encouragement:

> [We are] not to belittle God's discipline and not to lose heart in the face of God's rebuke. We should not see trials as cause for discouragement, but as a sign of God's determined love. We must reflect on the long-term benefits of our trials and recognize that discipline represents God's method of developing our maturity. We must respond to afflictions by searching out the faults or failures that hinder our spiritual growth.[2]

Let's use the wisdom of Hebrews 12:5 as our guide in taking advantage of the opportunity: "And have you forgotten the exhortation that addresses you as sons? 'My son, do not regard lightly the discipline of the Lord, nor be weary when reproved by him.'" This quote from Proverbs 3:11 contains the roadmap to this opportunity: the prospect of growing in our walk with Christ.

Do not regard lightly the discipline of the Lord. The one word in Greek translated "regard lightly" (*oligoreo*) means to believe something has little value. It is even translated "despise" in some English versions. If we are commanded in Hebrews to not regard lightly God's discipline, then the opposite is to regard it with importance. To put it another way, working through this may be the very thing God wants you to put at the top of your priority list right now. There may not be an observable

---

2   Thomas D. Lea, *Hebrews, James*, vol. 10, Holman New Testament Commentary (Nashville, TN: Broadman & Holman Publishers, 1999), 219.

cause-effect relationship that gives clarity to why you have been put in this position to suffer. Nevertheless, it is your wonderful opportunity for some self-examination. I am not saying this would be easy, but it will accomplish God's agenda of loving you into more Christ-likeness.

I would suggest you begin a journal or electronic document and work through the following questions:

- How have I reacted sinfully in any way to my circumstances?

- Who might have I offended in my reaction (regardless of whether or not I was treated justly)?

- What has my family observed in my reactions and responses?

- Have I shepherded my family through this crisis or have I left them to suffer alone while I focus on my own feelings?

- What have others said to me about myself that perhaps I have blocked out or blamed on them? Is there even a remote possibility that I did not see warning signs in my own conduct?

- Honestly, how God-directed have my thoughts and affections been? How much time and energy have I expended in seeking the Lord versus seeking justice?

- Who do I still need to forgive by confessing unforgiveness to God and acknowledging before the Lord that I forgive him/them?

- What input does my wife have to help me grow through this?

- What would I have done differently given another opportunity?

- What has this taught me about myself?

- What has this taught me about ministry and the church?

- How will I be different from now on?

- What Scriptures do I need to bring to bear in my own heart, perhaps to memorize to increase my sanctification in this area?

- What input might I get from concerned others who could shed light on how I might be more like Christ through this?

Do not be weary when reproved by God. The process of self-examination, while a difficult one, is an energizer to your faith. Don't fall for the trap that God's discipline wears you out; let the procedure of sanctification strengthen you and lift you up! As you work through this, the cry of your heart will be to praise God for His faithfulness to you! As you prayerfully seek God's wisdom to be a more gentle, kind, and humble man of God, He will draw near to you as you draw near to Him. These times of reflection will be precious to you in years to come. Set a schedule for yourself to work through these issues. Don't think that this will happen overnight. This is a process, but a worthy process.

Although it may be that you were completely innocent in the ministry disaster that happened to you, that is not the issue. The issue is taking advantage of the opportunity to increase in holiness and depth of maturity as a result of your trial. This journey will give you peace for your soul knowing you have done your best to follow the Lord. The resulting contentment you receive will satisfy you with a refreshing sense of gratification.

◆ ◆ ◆

Pastor Dan spent some time in prayer, then got up the nerve to call Mrs. Harper back the next day. "Mrs. Harper? This is Dan. I wanted to thank you for your phone call yesterday. I really needed that encouragement. I also want to thank you for your reminder to me that this is part of the Lord's discipline in my life. I was reminded from Hebrews 12 that God's discipline is a sign that I am His child and that He loves me. I will be doing some self-examination to take advantage of this opportunity."

Mrs. Harper replied with a warm tone, "I'm so glad to hear that, Pastor Dan—and you'll always be Pastor Dan to me." She continued, much to Dan's surprise, "You know, years ago when my husband left me, I had to do a lot of soul searching."

"When he *what?!*" Dan exclaimed.

"Well," Mrs. Harper chuckled, "I don't exactly talk to everyone about it. But one day I got home from running some errands with the kids, I was greeted by a note from George. It said something to the effect of, 'I can't take your temper and your mouth anymore. Let me know when you are ready to deal with it and I will come back home.'"

Refreshingly, for once, Dan was not thinking about himself right now. "What happened, Mrs. Harper?" Dan probed.

"First of all, I was so mad that I tore that note into a million pieces then proceeded to destroy a vase *and* kick the legs right out from under the coffee table. Then I broke down and spent the entire night crying. The next day I was so exhausted that I quickly got sick. I was so furious with George. I called one of my friends to help me get through this. She faithfully sat with me while I cried, yelled, ranted, and raved. For days, she spent every night with me to make sure I was okay. One day, my friend asked me a very difficult question: 'I know George should never have left, but does he have a legitimate complaint?' Pastor Dan, I began to search my soul. I began to realize that I was a very difficult woman to live with. I was continually nagging, complaining, and putting George down. I got mad at him for the littlest of things. The Lord was doing a wonderful work of showing me my own sin in the mirror of my husband. I asked my friend to arrange a meeting with George and I humbled myself with him and asked his forgiveness. Pastor Dan, without the Lord's discipline, I would still be trapped in that sinful pattern of thinking about myself all the time."

For Dan, who had gotten to know the tender character of Mrs. Harper and had observed her obvious love for her husband, the picture became clear. Mrs. Harper exhibited the precious uprightness today because of the Lord's discipline *yesterday*. With a breaking voice, Dan thanked Mrs. Harper for her transparency. Over the course of the coming weeks, Dan decided to do a self-inventory. As he was honest with himself, he began to see that those with whom he had ministered had become afraid to disagree with him because of his poor reactions. Finally, apparently one man had enough and decided to take Dan to task on it. He sent letters of apology to any he could remember he might have offended and asked for his wife's forgiveness as well. Although it did not immediately take away the pain of his circumstances, the relief he felt was palpable, and he knew that the Lord would help him move forward.

THE STUMBLING BLOCK

There is only one stumbling block that prevents us from gladly receiving the discipline of the Lord: pride. A pride based in the fear of what others might think and the fear that we may be falling short of the mark. The best response is given by Peter in 1 Peter 5:6, that you are to "humble yourselves, therefore, under the mighty hand of God so that at the proper time he may exalt you." Take heart and take hold of the Lord's hand. He won't let go.

A Prayer of Submission

Lord of All, I have been bought with the blood of Christ and You have promised to make me like Him. I embrace whatever trial You bring knowing that You will be faithful to me all the way home. Shine the light of Your holiness on the darkest places of my heart. Cleanse the recesses of my habitual sins and show me the way to consecrate my body to You. Let me be a living sacrifice and die to myself. Help me to forget what others may think and be only concerned with what You think. Help me to think your thoughts and to do your deeds. Should there be anyone with whom I must make amends, give me the courage and grace to do so for your glory. Make me more like Christ and give me the strength to bear up under your loving hand. All for the sake of giving honor to your name, Amen.

FORGIVE, FORGIVE, FORGIVE

In 2003, Gary Leon Ridgway, better known as the Green River Killer, confessed to the murders of 48 women. In 2011, Ridgway was convicted of the murder of Rebecca Marrero, bringing the victim count up to 49, but he believes it may have been as high as 60. At Ridgway's 2003 sentencing, the families of the victims had the chance to address Ridgway directly. Most were angry and lashed out at Ridgway for the grief he had put them through. As Ridgway listened to the family members express their grief and anger, he seemed unmoved. Then Robert Rule, the father of teenage victim Linda Jane Rule, came to speak. Rule said, "Mr. Ridgway . . . there are people here that hate you. I'm not one of them. You've made it difficult to live up to what I believe, and that is what God says to do, and that's to forgive. You are forgiven, sir."

The word "forgive" appears in your English Bible about 135 times. Forgiveness is life and breath to our faith. It is what we desperately need from God in order to be in right spiritual standing with Him. It is what we need and crave from those around us as our sin nature is continually showing itself. It is that which we are commanded by God to extend to those who have offended or hurt us. And forgiveness stands as possibly the most difficult action for a Christian to extend.

To forgive is easily the most beautiful and Christ-like action we will ever undertake as Christians. And for you who have been wounded and scarred in ministry by those whom you have loved the most, forgiveness is absolutely vital. You know well the little letter by Paul to Philemon, a letter imploring the Colossian church member to forgive the now-saved runaway slave, Onesimus. In the body of the letter, verses 8-18, we receive from the Scripture a model for forgiveness. Forgiveness requires supernatural help from the Lord, so I want to simply construct a prayer based on Philemon 8-18, a prayer to assist you in extending to others what Christ has already extended to you.

"Lord, I desire to obey Christ." In verse 8, Paul says that he is "bold enough in Christ to command you to do what is required." He had confidence based in his authority as an apostle that he could have simply commanded Philemon to forgive Onesimus. Jesus did, however, issue a direct command to forgive. When he commanded essentially unending, limitless forgiveness in Luke 17:3-4, the disciples said to him, "Increase our faith!" (v. 5). So Jesus gave the illustration of a servant doing what his master commanded regardless of what he felt like doing. The servant came in from a long day in the field, and the master commanded him to prepare the master's dinner, dress to serve dinner, and then wait on the master hand and foot until the master was satisfied. Jesus ended the story by reminding the disciples that their attitude toward forgiving others was to be: "We are unworthy

servants; we have only done what was our duty" (v.10). The first and foremost reason you are to forgive is because our Master has commanded it. Our prayer begins with the simple affirmation that we desire to obey Christ.

"...who has loved me with an everlasting love." In Philemon 9, Paul says that rather than giving the direct order, "yet for love's sake I prefer to appeal to you." Paul takes the softer road of appealing on the basis of love. He has a clearly established authority, yet he appeals to the transformative power of the gospel itself. Philemon had a choice and that choice was to be informed by his salvation. Having received the unmerited love, grace, and favor of God in that Christ paid the penalty for his sins, would he now *extend* grace or *withhold* grace? Ultimately, Paul's appeal "for love's sake" looks all the way back to the cross where love for Philemon was demonstrated to the greatest degree possible. Before you decide to withhold forgiveness, take a long look behind you at the blood still fresh on the cross—blood that was spilled for your forgiveness.

"With the same love, Christ died for _____ as well." You fill in the blank the person or persons whom you need to forgive. In Philemon 10, for the first time in the letter, Paul names the central character of the letter. He says, "I appeal to you for my child, Onesimus." This is the same Onesimus whom Paul speaks of as "our faithful and beloved brother" in Colossians 4:9. Paul then tells Philemon in verse 11 that "formerly he was useless to you, but now he is indeed useful to you and to me." Paul does not specify what he means by "useless." Perhaps he is referring to the wrong done to Philemon or

to the quality of Onesimus's work. It could even be referring to the crassness for which slaves in Philemon's region were known. The context makes the answer obvious, however. Previously, Onesimus was an unbeliever. He was "useless" in that he was spiritually dead and could not be a brother or fellow laborer in the gospel. But now, as a believer in Christ, Onesimus had become "useful." Paul is actually throwing in a little humor—never a bad idea in a tense situation—since the name "Onesimus" means *useful*.

As believers in Christ, we are "vessel[s] for honorable use, set apart as holy, *useful* to the master of the house" (2 Tim 2:21). To not forgive a fellow believer, regardless of how unfairly you may feel treated by him, is to treat someone as *useless* when God has proclaimed him *useful*.

"Use _____ mightily for your kingdom purposes." Paul's affection for Onesimus was obvious. He says in Philemon 12 that "I am sending him back to you, sending my very heart." Onesimus had endeared himself to Paul as a new brother in the Lord. But Paul had more than just brotherly affection for Onesimus; he had a real use and need for his services in the ministry. In verse 13, Paul said that he would have loved to have kept Onesimus with him "in order that he might serve me on your behalf during my imprisonment for the gospel." Onesimus was a slave; he was used to serving, but now with Paul his service had new eternal purposes. If Philemon were to hold a grudge for his own selfish ends, he would be taking out of service a key part of Paul's ministry. The decision to forgive Onesimus was not one in which Philemon would restore one relationship only, but a decision which

would impact the gospel work of the church. The person you may have something against is a vessel for God's use. Perhaps you think that person is not a very good vessel or very useful; that is not your call to make. Instead, pray earnestly that the kingdom might be advanced through that person's efforts. Or to put it another way, *put down your grudge and lift high the cross!* It is impossible to be upset with someone for whom you are praying to be used mightily by God.

"Give me a heart overflowing with grace and forgiveness to-ward _____." Now Paul focuses on Philemon himself. He says that he "preferred to do nothing without your consent in order that your goodness might not be by compulsion but of your own accord" (v. 14). Despite Paul's personal desires, he will defer to Philemon's judgment. Paul wants Philemon to extend forgiveness to Onesimus openly and with an overflowing heart. And this must be your prayer as well, that you might not begrudgingly slog through the mud of forgiveness, but rather have an abundant heart of grace characterized by a genuine eagerness to forgive.

"I acknowledge that you have sovereignly brought this trial for a purpose in my life and the life of others." In verses 15-16, Paul presents a hypothesis about the reason for the whole episode of Onesimus's escape, his subsequent contact with Paul, and his ultimate salvation in Christ. Paul says, that "perhaps this is why he was parted from you for a while, that you might have him back forever, no longer as a bondser-vant, but more than a bondservant, as a beloved brother." This is not addressing the issue of whether or not Onesimus would remain a slave. Rather, Paul is saying that Onesimus

is no longer *just* a slave, but *more* than a slave—a beloved *brother*! Paul is clearly acknowledging the mystery and heavenly purposes expressed by the sovereignty of God. For your trial in ministry, not only is God working out His perfect purposes in your life, but in the lives of every single person involved. This understanding helps grease the skids toward obedient forgiveness.

"Help me to demonstrate forgiveness toward _____ *with gracious loving actions."* After 16 verses, Paul finally makes his direct request of Philemon in verse 17: "So if you consider me your partner, receive him as you would receive me." In the context of first-century hospitality, the honor and virtue of this practice was that you received someone into your home in such a way that a stranger was treated as a member of the family—equal in status. Paul is asking Philemon to greet Onesimus in essence by saying, "My home is now your home." Dear brother, you must do the things that you do with a forgiven person. Even if someone has horribly offended you, reach out to him. Pray for him. As far as is possible, build every bridge possible. Your forgiveness is not just a state of mind; it is a call to action. Drawing near to the one who has offended you will remind you of the humanity and frailty of that person and also serve to remind you that you a lot more like *him* than you are like God. If circumstances prevent you from regular interaction, at the very least communicate your love and affection for this person in whatever form will express your warmth the best.

"I hold no debt against _____ *because you don't either."* In Philemon 18, Paul makes an astounding offer to

Philemon. He says that if Onesimus owes Philemon anything—perhaps from having stolen from him—"charge that
to my account." The only way that Paul could possibly have
known this was an issue was that Onesimus had apparently
confessed this to Paul. Whatever the debt was, Paul says that
he would repay it personally. This is explicit legal language.
Paul is writing Philemon an official promissory note for
Onesimus's debt to Philemon. Onesimus is no longer in the
equation. Paul agrees to pay the debt and in return Philemon
should agree to view Onesimus as clean and without blame.
There is an obvious gospel message imbedded in this trans-
action. We owed God the Father an unpayable debt because
of our sin, so Jesus took all that was owed and paid it on our
behalf with his very life so that we could be clean and without blame. The point is that *since God holds no debt against
the forgiven, neither can we.*

I might go so far as to say that I don't believe God will bless you
in ministry again until you have truly forgiven those who hurt
you. Not just a tentative obligation, but a genuine desire for them
to be used of the Lord for the greater kingdom purpose of building Christ's Church. If you are uncertain about the salvation of
one who offended you, since there are certainly tares among the
wheat, then you have all the more obligation to understand that
they were simply acting according to their nature. They need
the gospel, not your bitterness. For those you know who follow the Lord but simply went completely off-track in how they
treated you, your duty is clear: Forgive, forgive, forgive.

A Prayer for Help to Forgive

Lord, I desire to obey Christ who has loved me with an everlasting love. With the same love, Christ died for _____ as well. Use _____ mightily for your kingdom purposes. Give me a heart overflowing with grace and forgiveness toward _____. I acknowledge that You have sovereignly brought this trial for a purpose in my life and the life of others. Help me to demonstrate forgiveness toward _____ with gracious, loving action. I hold no debt against _____ because You don't either. In Jesus' name, Amen.

ASK FOR GRACE FROM THE LORD

Beneath the cross of Jesus I fain[3] *would take my stand*
The shadow of a mighty Rock within a weary land
A home within the wilderness, a rest upon the way
From the burning of the noontide heat and the burden of the day

Upon the cross of Jesus mine eyes at times can see
The very dying form of One Who suffered there for me
And from my stricken heart with tears two wonders I confess

The wonders of redeeming love and my unworthiness
I take, O Cross, thy shadow for my abiding place
I ask no other sunshine than the sunshine of His face
Content to let the world go by, to know no gain nor loss
My sinful self, my only shame, my glory all the cross

Elizabeth Clephane, the author of this 1868 hymn, "Beneath the Cross of Jesus," learned by her circumstances at an early age to cling tightly to the cross of Christ. She was a quiet child, dependent upon her parents, but she lost both at an early age. She had a tender heart of compassion and would minister

---

3 "Fain" is an archaic term which means "with pleasure" or "with delight."

comfort to those in need. "Among the sick and suffering, she won the name, 'My Sunbeam.'"[4] Elizabeth embedded a self-deprecating and God-glorifying message in the third verse of this hymn quoted above. Rather than receiving the glory for being a "sunbeam" she deferred this glory to God alone, "I ask no other sunshine than the sunshine of His face." In your time of great anguish, there is a child-like sense of relief in the thought of sitting under the cross's safe shadow. In seeing all other comforts stripped away, the "sunshine of His face" becomes crystal clear and the glory of the cross should overwhelm the soul.

I cannot speak for you, but in my own case, I literally felt betrayed by God when extreme ministry trials came upon me. Intellectually, I knew this was ridiculous, but it did reveal to me that I had certain expectations of God that were not accurate. After an intensive period of self-reflection, I came to the conclusion that my view of God had been too small and my view of myself had been too large. I came to realize that the so-called "disaster" was actually a magnificent gift from the Lord that radically improved my theology. I felt as small as an atom and God seemed so big that I could not grasp Him. Over the course of some months, I did begin to comprehend that this was a glorious place to be. So I repented to the Lord of my misconceptions of the magnitude of His Being and began anew to seek Him from the position of an atom-sized man approaching an infinite God. I began to ask for grace upon grace. I am not speaking of grace for salvation, but rather grace for living. Hebrews 13:9 exhorts us that "it is good for the heart to be

---

4 Robert J. Morgan, *Then Sings My Soul Book 2* (Nashville, TN: Thomas Nelson Publishers, 2004), p. 117.

strengthened by grace." The grace of God—His unmerited goodness toward us—is the source of our strength. The Spirit of God imparts the grace of God in many varied ways.

Our God is infinitely high and exalted. His holiness might be expressed by the idea: *there is God and there is everything else.* He is high above the heavens and completely sovereign over all. Yet, God became a man and walked through every possible trial. Jesus Christ knows every nuance of pain and anguish you have experienced. This is why Hebrews 4:15 is such a comfort to us, "For we do not have a high priest who is unable to sympathize with our weaknesses, but one who in every respect has been tempted as we are, yet without sin." There is nothing you are going through which Jesus does not understand perfectly. As a result, the following verse opens the floodgates to the grace of God: "Let us then with confidence draw near to the throne of grace, that we may receive mercy and find grace to help in time of need." "Confidence" is a word which means to come in a state of boldness in an intimidating situation. It implies courage with the expectation of receiving something good.

A Model for Seeking Grace

I want to use the prayer outline which Jesus taught His disciples in Matthew 6:9-13 as a guide for seeking the grace of God. This prayer is a comfortable place, and we are confident that we are praying rightly and within God's will when we utilize the Lord's example prayer. Let's apply this directly to your circumstances.

Our Father in heaven. Grab ahold once again to the remembrance that God is your Father. While I know this is Theology

101 to us, in a situation when it can feel like your Father has overwhelmed you with sorrow, it is imperative that we hold His hand once again. Feel the tender touch of His palm as He safely guides you through these treacherous waters of grief. Feel His strong hand on your back as He gently propels you forward toward the purposes He has always had for you.

Hallowed be your name. Contemplate the majesty of God. Dig out your theology works and read on the nuances of the glories of God. Remember His mighty power, His lovingkindness, His nature as Creator, His justice expressed in wrath to the unbeliever, His grace expressed in salvation for the elect. If necessary, write some essays on the attributes of God. Thank the Lord for His unfathomable infinite nature. Relish feeling the weight of His might next to the helplessness of your weakness. Certainly you have preached sermons on the glory of God—preach them to yourself now once again.

Your kingdom come, your will be done, on earth as it is in heaven. I take this quite literally, to pray for the consummation of God's kingdom. Your eschatological viewpoint doesn't make any difference here. Believers with every eschatological position all agree on one thing: we want the kingdom of God to come! This is an opportunity to receive the grace of God by remembering that you are only a minuscule part in the grand scheme of God's plan to bring His kingdom to earth. And yes, your ministry disaster was part of that plan. As you are reminded of the bigger design of redemptive history, you receive grace as you focus more on God's will and less on your part in it.

Give us this day our daily bread. The Lord knows what your immediate needs are right now. For many of you, ministry disaster may quite literally also mean financial disaster. It may mean a sudden change of employment for you. This can feel like your world has been turned upside down. You might have been delivering God's Word one day and delivering pizzas the next. You might have been studying the Scriptures one day and studying for an employment exam the next. Remember that God owns everything and He absolutely will not fail to take care of you. But more than just financial provision, God will also provide all the resources you need to get back on track emotionally as well. Ask Him for grace to provide all you need, then watch as your loving Father tenderly gives and gives and gives to you.

Forgive us our debts, as we also have forgiven our debtors. We find grace from God for the sins which muddy our boots in our walk with Him. We find the strength to confess our own sin and to let go of the sins of others. The grace given in forgiveness is like a spiritual vitamin shot for the soul. God's grace should put a spring in your step, that God is "faithful and just to forgive us our sins and to cleanse us from all unrighteousness" (1 John 1:9). What does this have to do with finding grace in the midst of ministry disaster? Your goal is not to fix the disaster—that is probably not going to happen. Your goal is to be a better man for it; your goal is to be fixated on holiness, for it is by this passion for God's holiness and your responsive holiness that you become the man God planned for you to be because of this very trial.

And lead us not into temptation, but deliver us from evil. Ask the Lord for grace not to go down the path of bitterness, anger, self-righteous justification, or vengeance of any kind. Ask Him to elevate your awareness of your own sin and to raise your awareness of ministry situations in which you will be most tempted to sin. For those of you who have already been honest with yourselves about your part in the ministry disaster, ask the Lord for the grace to never repeat those errors again.

A Time to Remember: An Official Starting Point

While we are called to be men of prayer marked by continual communion with the Lord, I want to encourage you to make preparations for one special time of prayer. This will be what we might call the official starting point of expectantly looking for the grace of God to manifest itself mightily in your life and situation. It will be a time to remember; it will be the moment you look back to a turning point. This is a time that should take you a half a day or more and will require some planning. Here are some suggestions to help you plan your meeting with the Lord to ask for grace:

- *Place*

  - Find a quiet place away from your home. If possible get outdoors into God's creation where you can meet with Him undisturbed.

  - This should be a place you can speak aloud to the Lord without fear of interruption or embarrassment. It should be a place where you can weep, sing, and shout if necessary!

- *Time*
  - I suggest early in the morning so that when you awaken this is immediately your focus for the day.
  - Give yourself plenty of time to get there and get home. Don't plan a lot of other things for that day.

- *Relational Preparation*
  - Get the support of your wife and family and ask them to pray for you.
  - Note that your wife may want in on this. That is your call. It may be that you need to do this alone first or that doing this together will be a major step forward for you.
  - Get the support of other believers by asking them to pray for you during that specific time.

- *Emotional Preparation*
  - Do not get distracted with other things prior to this special prayer time. On the day before start allowing your heart and mind to get more and more focused on what you are about to do.

- *Spiritual Preparation*
  - Begin praying about this time days in advance. Ask the Lord to prepare your heart to meet with Him in earnest. Know that He is looking forward to it!
  - If you feel compelled, you might even fast for a period of time prior to this time with the Lord.
  - Make a very specific order of events and focus points of your prayer. Prepare with all materials

you will need with you. Include thoughts from the model of the Lord's Prayer given above. Here is a sample order of events:

- » Opening prayer
- » Read Psalm 23 aloud and thank the Lord for it
- » Sing two hymns: _____ & _____
- » Prayer of praise: (have a prepared list to help get you started)
- » Prayer of confession
- » Prayer of thanksgiving for salvation and forgiveness
- » Sing a hymn _____
- » [AS NEEDED]—break for water, etc.
- » Opening prayer
- » Read Psalm 88 aloud
- » Prayer of Lament—cry out to the Lord with all the pain you have experienced. Speak to Pim as your Father.
- » Sing a hymn:_____
- » Prayer for grace—have a specific list of every single way you are asking the Lord to show his grace to you
- » Prayer for your wife and children—have a specific list of every request on their behalf
- » [AS NEEDED]—break for water, etc.
- » Opening prayer
- » Sing a hymn: _____
- » Read Psalm 150 aloud
- » Prayer of thanksgiving
- » Closing prayer

- *Physical Preparation*
  - Get a good night's sleep the night before. Get all the sleep you can.
  - Hydrate well in case this time with the Lord causes weeping.
  - If you are fasting up until this time, bring healthy snacks to end the fast.
  - You will be physically exhausted in all likelihood after this so make provision to get rest afterward.

Remember the details of this day. It will go down in history for you as a day you can look back upon as your official date of beseeching God's gracious favor in your life. Recall the words of the hymn:

I take, O Cross, thy shadow for my abiding place
I ask no other sunshine than the sunshine of His face
Content to let the world go by, to know no gain nor loss
My sinful self, my only shame, my glory all the cross

A Prayer for Grace and Mercy

God of grace, I kneel here before You as a broken man. I am nothing without Christ. I have endeavored to serve You and it seems that it was for nothing, yet I know You are working out your mighty purposes. Although I have not responded perfectly nor have I been sinless in this hour of trial, I am confident in your grace. I am asking You to do glorious and wonderful things through this trial. I am asking for an abundance of your lovingkindness and grace to cascade down into my life. I am asking that in the months and years to come I might look back at this trial and see your wisdom. I am asking that the blessings to come would completely overwhelm the pain I am experiencing now. And I ask that all this might be done to the ultimate glory of your grace and the honor of my Master, Jesus Christ. In His name I pray, Amen.

PRAYERFULLY LOOK AHEAD

I survived a car accident on a Dallas-area freeway. It happened right where the freeway split to go into two different directions. A car changing lanes in a desperate attempt to not miss his intended branch clipped my back bumper while swerving across to the left. The sideways force of the impact sent me immediately spinning clockwise in heavy traffic. For a split second, I was actually going completely backwards in my lane with enough time to look up to see the horrified face of the semi-truck driver next to me, eyes as big as softballs as he frantically maneuvered away from me. I then proceeded to keep spinning. By God's merciful hand, the final spin placed me facing perfectly forward in a grassy area off the left lane. Silence greeted me. No injuries; no collisions; no damage save a small dent in my bumper. I was fine. Now convinced that all was well, with great joy I got out of my vehicle . . . and proceeded to slump straight to the ground when my legs would not work at all. Unbeknownst to me, I had a physical reaction completely out of my control which rendered me as helpless as a baby for a couple of minutes.

This can be the same emotional reaction with men who have experienced ministry disaster. In the days and weeks following, they proclaim that they are okay. The Lord has sustained them and they are optimistic. But as time passes, they grow more introspective and even angry about what has happened. Thinking they were ready to get back into ministry again, they were not. More time was needed. If you are reading this just weeks after a ministry disaster, I implore you to let the Lord work in your heart over the course of time. You have been through the emotional version of a car accident. I am not in any way diminishing the faithfulness and power of the Lord to work; I am realistically assessing the certainty that traumatic events have traumatic consequences that take time to be worked out. Don't try to "jump back in the game" too soon. You have not had the time to reflect and assess what has happened yet. You need time to just "be" for a while.

When you work through the issues outlined in the rest of this book, there is a time and place to begin to foster hope for the future. As I stated in the introduction, you are a veteran of ministry and the church needs faithful shepherds. There is a high likelihood that you may be gun-shy. The pain you have experienced is not something you desire ever to experience again, and sadly, many men abandon the ministry because of this fear. But you and I both know that leadership in the church is a call from God. We are not talking about career options here; unless you have permanently disqualified yourself from church leadership (see Appendix A), you are compelled by God to serve Christ's church. It may be in a different church, a different city, a different state, or even in a different country—but you are compelled to serve. God gifted you for ministry and the church is starving for good men. I want to encourage you to begin to have hope for the future. There are some doubts you may be having and I want to give comfort to ease those doubts.

HOPE FOR THE FUTURE

You can love again. The fact is that part of what makes you "pastoral" is that God gave you a tenderness for people. You have no problem rejoicing with those who rejoice and weeping with those who weep. You have poured yourself into your people. You have officiated their weddings, buried their loved ones, baptized new believers, and worshipped the living God together. The fellowship of the church is the most unique fellowship on earth, forming a bond that is beyond our ability to understand. And it was some of these people with whom you bonded as shepherd who turned on you and who were suddenly filled with animosity toward you.

The Apostle Paul wrote to the churches of Galatia to confront their deviation from the gospel he originally preached to them. He was dismayed at their dismissal of the biblical gospel and he expressed this in terms of personal disappointment. In Galatians 4:13-14, he reminded them that he preached the gospel to them in the midst of a physical ailment. They had not only responded in salvation but had loved Paul, receiving him as if they were receiving Christ Himself. With obvious pain, he asked them, "What then has become of your blessedness…have I then become your enemy by telling you the truth?" (vv. 15-16). Paul is saying, "What did I do to deserve this treatment by you?" Paul had become vulnerable to love them and they had hurt him deeply.

The undershepherd of Christ's church is, by definition, a lover of the sheep. It is certainly tempting to withdraw from that arena and simply decide you will never get hurt like this again. But let me encourage you: there are other sheep, sheep you have yet to meet. And they will need your love and your shepherding. They won't see you as others have. The Lord will provide more sheep for you to love. And this time you will be even more effective because your love will be deepened by the scars you now bear. Rather than believing your ability to love is decreased, I assert instead that it will be *increased*. God will restore to you a group a people for whom you would join Paul in saying, "For God is my witness, how I yearn for you all with the affection of Christ Jesus" (Phil 1:8).

You can be loved again. There is the age-old debate about how close emotionally a pastor or elder should get with his congregation. Frankly, I cannot even believe that *is* a debate. I think that is an attempt by wary men to stay aloof and never get hurt. The fact is you cannot do effective ministry without getting vulnerable and getting real with those you shepherd. How can they learn to love like Christ unless they see it modeled in you, and *not* just from a distance? That being said, the aftermath of your trial may have led you to believe you are unlovable. Horrible descriptions of you may have been written, said aloud, or even published. Well, forget them! You are a child of the living God who bears the spiritual image of his Maker and who bears the fruit of the Spirit. You have been made by God specifically to shepherd His people. As you lovingly feed them the deep truths of the Word of God, they will love you and even feel indebted to you. After all, you are illumining to them the very

Savior they love and giving them a sneak preview of the heavenlies through the preached Word! You *can* be loved again, and by God's grace you will be.

God will use your trial for good. We have already dealt with the issue of the sovereignty of God in your trial, but I am not speaking now of your trial being used for *your* good, but for the good of others. The time of personal reflection and confession which you have been undergoing is having a marvelous impact on your heart: it is making you more like Christ. This can only benefit Christ's church (and frankly your family as well!). You will be more patient, more loving, more gracious and more sensitive in your ministry. You will take more time to nurture relationships and less time to rally the troops. You will lead more from your knees and less from the helm. You will see conflicts and trouble as glorious opportunities to do it better than you did before. And the end result is that a group of people, a local assembly of believers, will be blessed and love you as their wise shepherd. And now, your trial will have a new joy as you see it used not *just* for *your* good, but for the good of many others as well.

You will count yourself blessed for the experience. We all know the theory behind James 1:2-3, that the testing of your faith produces steadfastness and gives us reason for joy. Now you have the rare and blessed privilege to see this worked out experientially in your own life. To put it another way, you have the joy of seeing that the *outcome* of the trial made the trial all worth it. There will be benefits for your family, for your walk with the Lord, for your depth of wisdom, and for your ability as a shepherd. There *will* be a day—I repeat: there *will* be a day when you can honestly say to the Lord, "It was all worth it and I see the glory of your wisdom!"

DON'T FIGHT HOPE

When we were in the process of adopting our precious daughter, Julia, from South Korea, we endured quite an emotional roller coaster. With a normal pregnancy, timeframes are pretty clear: you won't be waiting longer than nine months. With international adoption, however, you spend what seems to be an eternity waiting and waiting. For us, we waited almost two years during the adoption process. One of the by-products of this process is the tendency to try to numb yourself—to stop hoping that the adoption could happen tomorrow. We discovered this phenomenon first-hand. In a conversation with a wonderful lady with our adoption agency, my wife expressed the challenge of waiting and how we were trying to not think about it. The woman simply said, "Don't fight hope." In other words, it was okay to hope that tomorrow could be the day!

There has to be a day in which you start thinking about getting back in the game, getting back behind the wheel, and every other over-used metaphor you can imagine. It may be that you are not ready for that day yet. If that is the case, then prayerfully put a date on your calendar when you *will* be ready and start working through the rest of the issues in this book with your eye on that date. Once you are committed to getting back to work for the Lord, then go all out. You are a different person now; you have the battle scars of ministry that have made you more like Christ. You have wisdom now you did not have before. You have a love for the sheep like never before. You have a love for God and his Word like never before. You have been made more fit than ever for ministry.

As an example, I now have a personal preference in the selection process for potential elders in our church. While we hold to all the biblical qualifications of an elder, I am hesitant to recommend we ordain an elder who has not been through a massively humbling life-changing experience. You simply can see the difference between the men who *have* and *have not* had to cry out to God in the midst of disaster. I look for broken men, men with scars, and men who have had tender faith beaten into them by the trials of life. And you are one of those men. You are one whom God has joyfully selected for *extra* pain and *extra* preparation and *extra* discipline. This should thrill your heart because God *never* wastes a trial; it is always for a purpose.

I close with the final paragraphs of the introduction:

> In his classic declaration of victory, the Apostle Paul proclaimed, "I have fought the good fight, I have finished the race, I have kept the faith" (2 Tim 4:7). Paul often used the metaphor of the athlete as a picture of the Christian life. He uses this metaphor specifically of the gospel ministry, however, in 2 Timothy 2:5. If you think you cannot bear any more pain or heartache, consider Paul who asserted, "I endure everything for the sake of the elect, that they also may obtain the salvation that is in Christ Jesus with eternal glory" (2 Tim 2:10). Paul considered himself a runner who would not quit until the race was won and he was home with the Lord.

The bottom line is that you must look in the mirror and tell yourself, "I am a minister of the gospel of Jesus Christ and I *must* run the race to completion." Gentlemen, the Church needs you to *run again.* You might be running wounded, but you must run, nevertheless. Get to the starting line—the gun is about to go off and you need to be ready to burst off the starting blocks when it does.

A Prayer of Hope for the Future

Sovereign Lord over my life, I'm ready. Use me at your good pleasure. Let me run in the name of the Lord and use the precious lessons You have taught me for the good of Christ's Church and for your glory. I will await your command. In Jesus name, Amen.

Appendix A

Dealing with Complete Ministry Disqualification

You may be one who has completely disqualified himself from ministry as an elder or vocational pastor-elder. You were unfaithful to your wife or did something that is in reality unrecoverable in regards to the 1 Timothy 3 qualifications. You know it and other mature believers have affirmed it, but this does not mean that God is finished with you. There are some positive steps you can take to be a faithful steward of that which God has left you.

1. Prayerfully find a church that is governed by a godly group of qualified elders. If you were pastoring in a church and the offense took place in that context, it is probably best to start fresh in a new assembly. This is not just so you can get a fresh start but so the church you were in can get a fresh start.

2. Through whatever means the elders dictate, give them the honest truth about your situation. Ask them if they would consider acting as or assigning a loving advisory council. The job of this council would be to understand your situation and come up with a long-range plan to eventually allow you to serve at whatever non-elder role they deem appropriate. I realize there is a wide variety of

understandings of precisely what constitutes disqualification and precisely what level of ministry a disqualified man might do. Therefore, submit to the wisdom of the elders of the church. If the elders, however, want to "fast-track" you and minimize the seriousness of your offense, politely ask them to take this more seriously.

3. Serve at whatever level the elders allow and at whatever pace they dictate. If they say that they are only comfortable with you folding church bulletins for a year, then fold with excellence and joy, praying for every person who will receive one. Accept the will of the elders as the will of God (Matt 18:18) and rejoice in the clarity you have received. Make it your aim to do the most menial and lowly tasks possible. You will find a wonderful satisfaction in being the lowest.

4. Make your family a major focus. Without a doubt, those closest to you will be the most hurt. They need you, your time, and your full attention. Make a plan with your wife to have significant amounts of time with her and with your family as a whole. Make plans to spend individual time with each of your children.

5. Be an encouragement to others. While you may not occupy the pulpit, sit on the church eldership, or have authority in the church, you can still be a source of light and joy to every person with whom you come in contact. The Lord's joy is not exempt in your life. Joy is available to each and every believer and it can be your mission to spread as much of it as possible.

Appendix B

The Wife of the Shepherd

While this book has been directed at men in the ministry, I want to speak for a moment to their wives. You have been there for every moment of the agony and humiliation. You have suffered in ways even your husband has not. You have possibly struggled with embarrassment and even having a decreased trust in your husband. I want to give some proactive principles that may help you walk through this trial.

1. Remember that if you fall apart emotionally, your husband is now trying to pick up his own pieces and yours at the same time. He may not be strong enough yet to do this. It is vital that you maintain an energetic walk with the Lord personally. Your prayer life and time in the Word should be heightened during this time. As often as he has been strong for you, this may be a time when you must be strong for him. You may literally be the only person with whom he can be totally open and honest right now.

2. Pray for your husband more than ever before. He is struggling with feelings of abject failure. He is fighting sinful tendencies such as bitterness and anger. He needs supernatural support. Spend time in prayer and even in fasting on your husband's behalf and let him know you are doing so. He needs all the spiritual support he can get.

3. If your husband seems distant, be patient with him. He is working through what may be the hardest trial of his entire life. Men are not great multi-taskers and his ability to love you may seemingly be dampened. While I don't ever want to give a man an excuse for being an unloving husband, the fact is that the sheer mental and emotional distraction is overwhelming for him. Be patient and wait upon the Lord as you encourage him.

4. Encourage your husband with simple things a man relates to—a great meal, a night out, a surprise time of intimacy, a trip to the shooting range, tickets to a movie, and so forth. He needs to be reminded to enjoy the life God has given him.

5. Let God be the main tool to sanctify your husband during this time of self-reflection. In all likelihood, he has had numbers of people beating up on him. He may have literally lost all his closest friends, at least for the time being. The last thing he needs is the person closest to him to heap on more criticism. Even if the ministry disaster was totally his fault, short of him completely denying any responsibility, give him over to the Lord. You just love him unconditionally. Never view him as or tell him he is a failure or that his life is worthless. In these situations, it is sometimes the wife who becomes the greatest thorn in the side simply out of her own anguish.

6. Read the chapter on the sovereignty of God and take the principles to heart. It will give you a longer-view perspective on this trial.

Appendix C

Communicating Your Position without Blame or Aggressive Defense

This is an addendum to Chapter 2, "What You Must Stop Doing: Defending Yourself." There may be a time in which it is appropriate to communicate your position to relevant parties. It may be that you have been accused of something that is blatantly untrue with no grain of truth to it. Prayerfully, you may need to state the truth for the sake of your own conscience and to make sure that others have all relevant information. Here are some principles to consider when crafting this written position in letter form.

- Explain the purpose of the letter in humble terms
- Leave out emotionally charged words
- Never completely deny accusations of internal sinful attitudes
- Acknowledge all grains of truth in any accusation
- Only provide your position on completely black and white external issues that are clearly false—do so in very humble and deferential ways
- Never accuse others

- Never make yourself look like a hero
- Be clear that you are not asking for any actions or acknowledgements
- Do not try to gain sympathy or pity—this will likely have the opposite effect
- Give God all glory
- Do not be self-righteous and look down upon those to whom you are writing
- Acknowledge your genuine love for the recipients and your hope for future restoration and reconciliation.

Now, let's examine these principles in two sample letters, one less effective and one more effective and pleasing to the Lord. I am using the example of a pastor who mismanaged church funds.

Principle	Less Effective Letter	More Effective Letter
Explain the purpose of the letter in humble terms	Dear_____, I am writing to rectify a false accusation against me.	Dear_____, I am writing to give a simple clarification to one issue in particular. This is for the sake of truth, and not for the sake of defending myself.
Leave out emotionally charged words	I am shocked and humiliated that such horrible thoughts about me were even considered.	I will be brief and am hopeful that this information will be considered.
Never completely deny accusations of internal sinful attitudes	You have accused me of handling this situation pridefully. Well, if I had done anything wrong, I would have reason to be humble, but I have done nothing wrong.	First of all, I have been told that I have reacted very pridefully to this situation. I am certain that I could have demonstrated more godliness and less selfishness. Thank you for the feedback.
Acknowledge all grains of truth in any accusation	[In a less effective letter, there is a noticeable absence acknowledging truth]	In the first place, I see now that as pastor, I should not have been handling the financial books of the church. This is not my greatest skill nor did I have all the knowledge necessary pertaining to sound church financial practices that I should have. As a result, money was unaccounted for and expenses were not properly handled. I should have had much more accountability and frankly should have had others doing this work.

Principle	Less Effective Letter	More Effective Letter
Only provide your position on completely black and white external issues that are clearly false. Do so in very humble and deferential ways	I can't believe you would accuse me of stealing! Okay, so I'm not the greatest book-keeper in the world but this does not make me a thief!	As a further result, it certainly looked as if I had misappropriated church funds. While I have no way to prove otherwise, my conscience is clear in that I never intentionally misused funds. Had I the opportunity to do it all over again, I would have turned the finances completely over to a team designated by the elders. Because I did not take this step, funds were not all tracked or accounted.
Never accuse others	If Jack would have looked at the books like he was supposed to none of this would have happened!	I alone am responsible for this error in judgment.
Never make yourself look like a hero	I have done everything in this church! I preach, teach, counsel, keep the books, and clean on Saturdays. I have worked my fingers to the bone in this ministry.	I should have listened to the counsel you gave me earlier.
Be clear that you are not asking for any actions or acknowledgements. That is the Lord's work.	I demand an apology for smearing my reputation. If you were righteous men, you would all step down for your mistreatment of me.	I am not asking for anything whatsoever, but simply hoped you would prayerfully consider these words.

Principle	Less Effective Letter	More Effective Letter
Do not try to gain sympathy or pity. This will likely have the opposite effect.	I have sobbed myself to sleep every night for a month. I have lost weight and can't focus on anything. I can't believe how unfair you have been to me.	The Lord has been very gracious and kind to me and for that I am very grateful.
Give God all glory.	You will have to live with the fact that you took away my church.	Even in my lack of wisdom in this area, I believe God will be glorified and this is my prayer.
Do not be self-righteous and look down upon those to whom you are writing.	I am praying for you men to finally show some wisdom. I have done nothing wrong and therefore have nothing to confess.	I am grateful that you took time to read this and hopeful that it may give you some peace of mind.
Acknowledge your genuine love for the recipients and your hope for future restoration and reconciliation.	I thought you were my genuine friends, but I guess I was wrong.	I have a genuine affection for each of you and am hopeful that the Lord will allow me to regain your trust and affection in the future.